Copyright © 2019 by Courtney Alex Aldor

All rights reserved. This book or any portion thereof may not be reproduced or used in any manner whatsoever without the express written permission of the publisher except for the use of brief quotations in a book review.

Printed in the United States of America,
First Printing, 2019

ISBN 978-0-578-58722-6

www.CourtneyAlex.com

Trust Your Magical Self!

...how to be super PSYCHIC, extra INTUITIVE, and love your SENSITIVE soul

courtney alex kedor

FOR:
MOM
MAMU
CLARA
EVELYN
& PEARL

If we see ourselves as having failed, then we block our ability to succeed. Nothing in this world ever happens by accident...

   --the Unknown ;)

contents:

IN THE BEGINNING...

Your Very Real, Very Available Superpowers......27

What Is Intuition, Exactly?......28

So, How Did I Get Here?...... 32

P.S. This Book Came Through Intuition......35

How To Use This Book + A Lil' Disclaimer......36

SECTION 1: GETTING CLAIR

CHAPTER 1: FEAR VS INTUITION

When Fear Of Intuition Blocks Your Intuition...(Seriously, That's A Thing)......43

Fear Vs. Intuition......44

Shedding Light On Fear:

   * Fear Of Being Wrong......52

   * Fear Of Needing To "Protect" Ourselves......53

   * Fear Of Being Too Energetically Sensitive......54

   * Fear Of Perceiving Too Much......56

Kasia & The Legs......57

Subtle Energy Science, Genetic 1's & 0's......58

AND...Now Back To Kasia & The Legs......59

CHAPTER 2: SELF-TRUST

Sally Eats Lunch In The Alley......65

On Self-Trust:

   * Honesty......67

   * Surrender......69

   * Trusting Past Mistakes......71

   * Trusting In The Order of Things......74

   * Re-Building Trust......75

 The Dreaded Maybe's......78

INTUITION 101: YES/NO ANSWERS......79

Defining Maybe......81

What If You're Just Making It Up?......78

Giving Yourself Permission......78

All Are Called, Few Choose To Listen. BUT...How Do We Listen?......81

CHAPTER 3: THE CLAIRS

On Becoming Egg-Voyant......85

So, Is Being Egg-Voyant A Thing Then?......86

The Clairs:

  * Clairvoyance......88

  * Clairaudience......89

  * Clairsentience......90

  * Claircognizance......91

  * Clairgustance......91

  * Clairsalience......92

  * Clairempathy......92

Putting It All Together......93

CLAIR COUSINS: Mediumship, Remote Viewing, Channeling, Dreaming & Reading Anything...From Our Pets To Akashic Records!:

  * Mediumship......94

  * Channeling & Telepathy......95

  * Remote Viewing, Astral Travel, Dreaming & Reading Anything, Really......96

Phone Troubles......98

SO...Let's Play With Energy!......99

ENERGY TOOL #1: Plugging In Your Energy......103

Did Anyone See Christopher Columbus Sailing The Ocean Blue?......107

CHAPTER 4: CLAIR-ING YOUR LENS

Reading Through A Smudgy Lens......111

Energetic Filters & Blocks:

  * Finding Energy Blocks: Stories, Ideas, Beliefs......113

  * Finding Energy Blocks: Projection......115

  * Clearing Projections, Ideas, Beliefs & Stories......116

  * Finding Energy Blocks: Unexpressed Emotion......118

  * Clearing Energy Blocks In The Emotional Body......119

* Finding Energy Blocks: Stagnant Energy In the Physical Body......129

* Clearing Energy Blocks In The Physical Body......131

* Finding Energy Blocks: Stagnant Energy In Your Living Space......134

* Clearing Energy Blocks In Your Living Space......134

Leaving Your Body......138

Reclaiming Your Own Energy......139

Calling Back Your Energy......139

ENERGY TOOL #2: Calling Back Your Energy......141

Uncovering Your Hidden Gems......144

CHAPTER 5: CLAIMING YOUR SUPERPOWERS!

Spiros In Spirit......149

Yin & Yang: Shadow & Light......151

Shadows & Blind Spots......154

Entities......155

"Taking On" & Giving Away" Energy......158

...And Now A Bit On Boundaries......164

ENERGY TOOL #3: Creating A Separation Object......169

Hades & Persephone......171

SECTION 2: WORKING YOUR VOYANCE

CHAPTER 6: ENERGY READING 101

Now For The Fun Part :) 177

Kelly & Her Meditation......178

ENERGY TOOL #4: Centering......181

Reading Energy......185

ENERGY TOOL #5: Energy Reading, Flower Technique......187

ENERGY TOOL #6: Energy Reading, Stick-Figure Technique......193

Tips For Best Results In Energy Reading......196

Eyes Open Vs. Closed......196

AAAND...Practice Of Course......197

Your Energy Language Library......198

Grandma V......196

Energy Reading, Eyes Open......197

ENERGY TOOL #7: Reading Yourself, Eyes Open......199

My First Reading......202

CHAPTER 7: READING YOUR GUIDES

The World Wide Web Of Trees......207

Spirit Guides & Guidance......208

ENERGY TOOL #8: Reading Your Guides......211

Angels, Ancestors, Guides & "Dark" Energies:

　* Angels......216

　* Guides......217

　* Ancestors......218

　* "Dark" Energies......220

Raising Your Vibes......222

Ocean In View, O The Joy!......222

How To Get Daily Messages From Your Guides......224

Calling In Guides For Reading Energy......225

CHAPTER 8: READING OTHERS

Reading Other People......229

On Ethics......231

Rob & Bob & Friday Night......233

ENERGY TOOL #9: Flower Reading For Other People (Even Pets!)......237

Justine & Her Crush......240

ENERGY TOOL #10: Closing A Reading......245

Say What You See, A Note On Interpretation......248

Stage Fright: What If Nothing Came At All?......248

CHAPTER 9: ADVANCED TOPICS IN ENERGY READING

Petra & Her Pet Fish......253

On Intention......254

Reading Relationships......255

ENERGY TOOL #11: Flower Reading For Relationships......263

ENERGY TOOL #12: Career Reading......269

ENERGY TOOL LUCKY #13: Psychic Reading – Predictions & Time......273

Channeling......276

Akashic Records & Life Purpose......277

Baby Spirits......277

Ascended Masters, Mentors & "Trying On" Energy......278

Letting Your Voice Go Free......279

Chessa & Her New Job......280

CHAPTER 10: TAKING YOUR PSYCHIC SKILLS TO THE WORLD!

Daniela & The Shapeshifter......285

Tarot, Crystals & The World As Your Energy Library......286

Expanding Your Energy Library......287

Your Energy Library Out In The World......291

Manifestation Vs. Confirmation......294

The Charge......296

Definite Confirmation: A Sign, A Symbol......296

Energy Maps: Chakras, Meridians & More......298

Shifting Your Reality From The Inside, Manifesting Anything......299

Follow Your Feet, Follow Your Intuition......303

IN THE END...

The 4,000 Page Book With All The Answers......307

Little Miracles......308

Amplifying Energy Together......310

How Do I See?......311

How Do You?......312

This Book Was Completed Through Intuition......313

APPENDIX

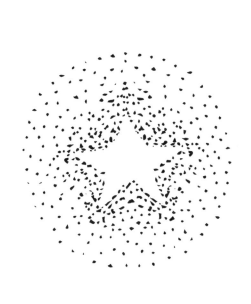

When I first started this project, I **did it** to soothe my soul. Although I didn't know it at the time, I now see I needed **to** understand my version of the world, to filter this experience into words **somehow.** That is, one of just knowing things I haven't been told without any idea **how** I know, I just do. Of sometimes seeing past, present, and future all at once. **Of** hearing a person's words while noticing something like a movie play behind **their** head...which doesn't always sync up with what they're saying, mind you. **Of being** able to lean on this table my laptop happens to be sitting on, while it — **the table**, that is — tells me the story of how it was made, that it has been cherished **and** loved. And all this because I happen to be sensitive, a trait I've spent a long **time** trying to comprehend.

You see, I grew up with the message **that there**'s something screwy or even difficult about being a daydreamer, empath, **channel,** psychic, medium, or all-around sensitive soul. But, to me, being sensitive means receptive and perceptive, in tune with all that is — even, and especially, **with** what the eyes cannot see. If I were to go to a doctor, they might say I'm **someone** who tunes out, can't focus, dissociates sometimes — which sounds like **a disease** in need of a cure. And it's funny because that's exactly how I came to realize what kind of gift was bestowed upon me...and all of us humans, really, when we open up to our superpowers through realizing all the ways we thought we were just making it up. This all started with a headache. But more on that in a sec.

I'll give you the example that comes up time and again when someone is speaking to me and suddenly asks where I've gone. What happens, when someone's words don't quite match their energy, is that I go "out." To find truth, that is. To the bigger, broader picture. Which usually resembles an actual picture that looks to me like an alternate reality happening just behind the hair on a person's head. Yup. It's not that I can't focus, listen, pay attention, or hear — it's more like I can hear it all. Or at least I'm hearing different aspects of whatever *it* may be. And I know I'm not the only one. Does this ever happen to you? If so, I hope you're wanting to scream at the top of your lungs with me. Or maybe you're holding back because you don't want to disturb the energies. And I hope that maybe it even happens a few more times throughout the course of this thing that has been, for me, somewhere along the lines of a personal unfolding, a writing of my own manual for living life on the sensitive side and...well, I don't even know what. I'll leave some of that to you. But it has been a totally transformative, if not completely wild experience that I'd definitely recommend.

This book is dedicated to all of you who cry for no good reason, enjoy a good song so much you can taste it, sit at the kids' table because somehow it just feels better, and dance like maniacs because you couldn't stop the immensity and intensity of love that flows through you if you tried.

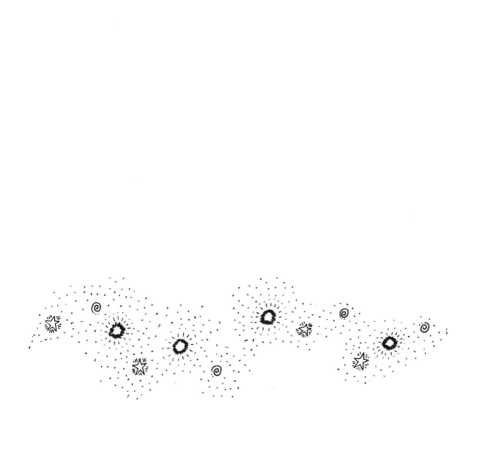

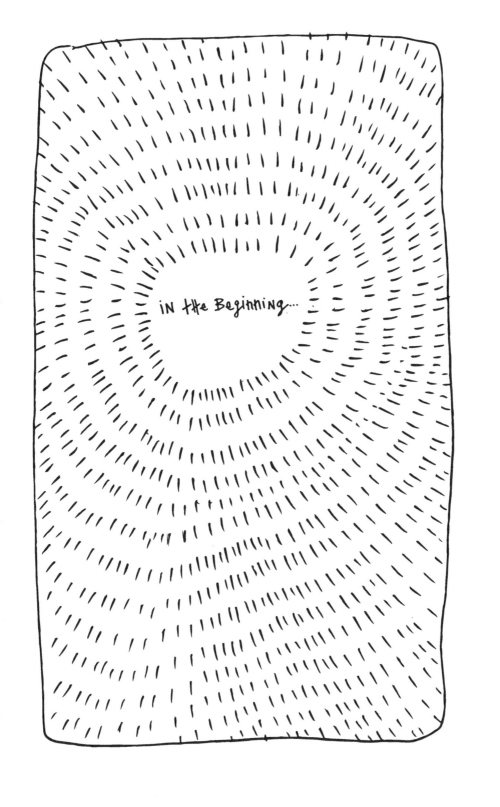

Your Very Real, Very Available Superpowers

It was springtime in Brooklyn and I was volunteering at a kids' superhero story-writing workshop when something super-heroic happened. Sitting at the back of the class, I was running the projector machine as a group of 3rd graders sat up front. Sue was leading the workshop, teaching the kids about character writing, asking them to shout out some superhero traits for the lead. "Super strength!" one kid shouted. "Flying!" screamed another. "Speaks Chiineeeese....?" The kids burst out laughing. I looked up at the back of their heads. *How about psychic?* I thought. One of the quieter boys put up his hand, "How about psychic?" He said. Sue wrote it down as the class let out an "Ooooooh!" I perked up in my seat and wondered if I could make it happen again. *Mmmm...what if they had telepathy?*, I thought. Soon, a small girl echoed it out loud, "Mmmm...what if they had telepathy?" The kids looked impressed. So was I, but for an entirely different reason.

Like me, you've probably dreamt of waking up to discover you have superpowers. But what if you suddenly realized you came equipped with them at birth, even if you were never given the manual? What if, in feeling so super powerful, you realized you were all-knowing too, but just hadn't had permission to say so?

What if you finally admitted, even if just to yourself, that you're able to communicate with the unseen world, download all the information you could ever need — without having to consult your phone — in order to live your happiest, healthiest, most purpose-driven and all-out magical life? What if you had more clarity about what you do and why?

I can pretty much guarantee that if you happen to be holding this book in your hands, your system of guidance is trying to speak to you RIGHT NOW. Tons of information on whatever's most in need of your precious attention — even to do with things happening miles away — is just waiting to come through via your intuition, your innate ability to channel, to receive guidance through your acutely tuned psychic lens, whether that be your clairvoyance, clairaudience, empathy, telepathy, subtle sensitivity, or another way in which you've been gifted at picking up on what we'll simply refer to here as energy. Can you hear it now? It's okay if it's fuzzy or has seemingly turned out to be wrong in the past, confused with fear or mistrust or some other annoying version of "maybe" or "but what if I should" type of talk. That's what we're here for. And while that reason may not be specifically to communicate telepathically with eight-year-olds, we're going to talk about why you probably already can. Yes, that's right, we're talking everything and anything psychic, empath, tarot, channeling, dreaming, medium-ing, remote viewing, clairvoyance-ing, mental downloading...everything that's got to do with how we humans can all naturally read and share energy. And while this stuff will become more clear as you get on with this book, know that I'm going to use a lot of these words interchangeably, because they all come through the vehicle of sensitivity and intuition. So, on that note, let's start there.

What Is Intuition, Exactly?

If you Google the word "intuition," you'll find a definition that refers to a hunch or a clue that logic can later test out. And while I love that explanation because it sounds so common, so easy, so much like nothing...well, I wonder if that's why we've also been treating it as such. If you think of the times you've had a truly mystical experience with intuition, can you relate to such a simple description?

As I got deeper into the topic, I realized I was still struggling to explain the greater details of my intuitive knowings, what to do with them, why I received certain bits of information in the first place. And I didn't have many words to describe how they were coming through in my daily life, beyond terms like "seeing," "hearing," "I've just got a gut feeling," "goosebumps," and "I don't know, I just followed my heart and the flow brought me here." While it was all true, it never fully described the extent of it. Maybe the closest example would be that it was like an antenna picking up random pictures and sounds. Of course, I wondered what to do with all the information, when to act on it, speak it out loud, surrender to the waters that were swirling around me, or take hold of the steering wheel and say to myself, *Thanks but no thanks, I'm going to steer this ship in a different direction today*. How could I know when to trust these "knowings," when to give them more thought, and when it was best to just notice and let them pass me by? And then there were other questions, like how do I communicate intuitive hits I get to my boss or my logic-loving family, who likes to refer to me as the artsy one?

Because if a hunch refers to something not yet proven, not concrete or material — and let's face it, we in the West live in a material-focused world — that means our hunches and intuitions have taken a back-seat role up until now. So it's no wonder that, in general, most of us have considered or come to rely on our intuition only somewhat. It makes sense that until now, we've had reason to turn down the volume on what we can only sort of explain, to instead focus on what can be seen, heard, touched, tasted, smelled, and talked about. While we have many words to describe the stuff of the "formed" world, we've seemingly focused a little less on the...uh, less formed. See? I don't even have a good English word to describe that. And so, for me, the process of honing my intuition to that of a finely tuned GPS, of gaining more insight and tapping into my own psychic realms with greater trust and more ease, has involved expanding my library a little. It meant giving voice to what I can now proudly admit I have always sensed. And in that, I learned to put more faith in and build trust in the intricate details of those things I only metaphorically "see."

Like a school of fish swimming in unison must perceive and therefore intuit much information about the direction of water flowing around them, we humans ought to be able to tap into the subtleties of whatever's going on around us — which, for now, we're just going to call energy. And so, for the next bunch of pages, we little fishies will be focused on using our intuition to read those energies in all forms, in a bunch of different ways, so that together we can come to a greater understanding. And if you're not yet convinced about "energy," I invite you to call it whatever you like. Ancient traditions have used terms like Qi, Ki, Prana, Life-Force...some of us really like to call it the Universe, but even a fun nickname will do. That part doesn't matter so much as describing the experience of perceiving it, because that's how we develop a closer relationship with it.

While certain abilities related to intuition have, in the last 100 years or so, been referred to as paranormal, they're really more like totally normal. Contrary to what you may have seen in Hollywood, not everyone's psychic sense looks like a perfectly clear movie that appears in the center of their head. You don't need a costume or a magic pill to access it, and you might never see rings of colored light around your friends. Sorry. But the good news is, when you sharpen your unique and God-given skills — the ones that were designed to help you with anything from relationship and career stuff to life-purpose guidance from your spirit team — it is super freaking helpful day to day. Animals use their instincts to, say, know who's most likely to feed them under the table at a dinner party — so why shouldn't we? And the coolest part is, when you can sense your own perception of energy, you have the power to make quick shifts in your own energy field too, to manifest with greater ease. Why? Because in order to manifest all we want, all we have to do is dissolve the blocks that have us believing we can't. And we'll get to that.

I'll also remind you that we all have our own ways of using our intuition, of picking up on energy signals. No two people are the same. While I might "see" and "know" stuff, my friend might tap more into her sixth sense when she sits down to draw or write. If you're a dancer or athlete, your body sensations may give you the strongest clues. And if you love music, you might suddenly hear lyrics to a song that just pop into your head with answers to the questions you've been needing answers to. There are just so many ways to get messages. And in the next chapters, we'll talk about how to develop a lot of those skills — from ones you already knew you had to those you didn't.

What if you already hear your angels, get messages from friends and spirit guides when the clock strikes 5:55, and see signs everywhere? That's great! The world contains a language of energy that goes well beyond words. One of my mentors often says the reason we love sacred geometry, crystals, pictures, symbols, artistic expression, and even tarot and other forms of tapping into higher energy is because our English language is so limited in its description of such. So we're going to dive deeper into that, whatever *it* may be, by developing our energy library for getting even more detail about our intuitive hits. For instance, I know that seeing 5:55 brings me messages related to harmony and tells my friend Anna about her ex-boyfriend, while it probably means something totally different for you. Also helpful is understanding whether you're tapped into one of your guides or just a really bossy great-great-grandmother. And on that note, can you ask deceased family members to shush it? Why, yes, you can. Can you call in that sort of help from the "unknown"? Yes, that too. And all of it via intuition.

Having a strong sense of intuition also means being willing to look at our blocks. It's seeing everything that's on the path in front of us, even the boulders. When that happens, when we can see all of ourselves, intuition starts to guide us in its purest form, with little to no effort. So, to develop our gift for clear and intuitive sight, or clairvoyance, we also have to work on removing the gunk that's been smudging up our lens. Once we clean the filters, so to speak, we can connect to our inner wisdom more clearly — whether you see, hear, feel or even taste it. For intuition is how we connect with the voice of deep inner knowing, at once aligned with our unique purpose and individuality, while equally connected to the truth and oneness of all that is. I have personally found that I'm able to connect to it with ever more ease, strength, and trust as I get more practice reading energy, because it's meant learning to pay as much attention to the formless (or inner) world as the ever-popular formed (or outer) one we all know so well. And so, throughout this book, we're going to talk about how to do that, with stories, tools, exercises, and more. We'll start off by talking about how we're all intuitive, why we sometimes block our full intuitive potential, and what to do about it. Later, I'll give you a bunch of different tools for reading and clearing energy. By the end of the book, you'll be so super pro at it and have undeniable solid proof of your expert psychic senses from the most knowledgeable person in the room — you.

So, How Did I Get Here?

Why all the intuition and psychic stuff and mediums and empaths and sensitivity and energy talk anyway? Well, I've come to realize, through a roller coaster of a ride, that they're all kind of one and the same. And that when you're born "sensitive" like so many of us are — like half of us, actually — you're naturally pretty good at some or all of the above. Truly, all humans have the capacity for these gifts, some just have to work a little harder at it. And while there are those who grew up with the knowledge and support for how to get through everyday life while incorporating the more, uh, subtle realms, I, for one, did not. No, I was never taught the difference between angels and guides, or that you don't always need to listen to your ancestors, even if they are in spirit. And for that matter, no one ever told me how to choose my spirit friends like I lovingly select the ones in human or animal form.

I was told, and often not in so many words, that having a sensitive nature was going to be hard. That competition and leadership and doing lots is great, while rest, receptivity, and caring kindly about others and my environment are also fine, but those things aren't really what's going to help me get ahead in life. And while logic prevails, belief in "the Universe" and such is okay, so long as it helps with all the more important stuff we all came here for, like buying insurance.

I was born to immigrant parents. Funny, but my maternal grandmother is actually from Transylvania. And once my family came west to Canada, the main goal was simply to survive and fit in. So, basically, no one ever taught me how to deal with my possible vampire lineage. In fact, my mom lovingly suggested I leave that last part out. I learned early on that my strange gift for "knowing" and speaking things out loud was not my friend, even if those things sounded like totally valid truths to me. It meant saying inappropriate-sounding things like, "It's good that Daniel's sick because there's a lesson to be learned from it," was usually met with cold stares, subjects changed, and sometimes even a scolding from one of the adults or the more socially savvy kids in the room.

Growing up, I had an annoying talent for knowing, and voicing, things about the adults in my life. If my single dad was going out to see his girlfriend but told me he was going to the store to pick up milk and would be back soon, I'd ask innocently why he was going to tuck another girl into bed. I often knew the truth of a matter, the energy underlying it, even if I couldn't fully grasp it. And I could feel other people's feelings — my dad's annoyance at this, for example — sometimes stronger than my own, and even if they weren't around. I heard thoughts that didn't sound like mine. I dreamt of and sometimes saw future events. Even if it was something so simple as waking up singing a song that would eventually play once someone turned some music on. I was one of those kids with a cold room who knew it meant there were definitely ghosts in her closet even when my parents told me such things didn't exist. Well, yeah, not in human form. My super duper specialty, even to this day, is accidentally triggering the s*^t out of someone by saying the very thing they'd rather leave unsaid. A spiritual gift, I suppose, which might be good for helping to heal our collective humanity or something but totally sucked in high school. And so I developed a kind of fear around this stuff, a serious case of self-mistrust.

Eventually, it manifested as chronic migraine headaches — the result of trying to shut my third eye. By my early 20s, the pain was fierce. I knew taking pills wasn't good for me, so I searched for a cure. It led me down a path of learning about holistic health, listening deeply to my body in order to get well. I read countless books on food, exercise, herbs, and lifestyle, and I took all sorts of healing workshops. Ever try rolling around on the floor speaking Japanese, even though you don't know any, just because you've been told it might help you align more deeply with yourself? I have. And while these things helped somewhat, an important piece was missing.

One Sunday, my friend was bringing his new girlfriend, Sherry, by for brunch. I'd met her a couple of times before. They were really late, they didn't text or call, but I knew they were still going to come. I noticed I started cooking more food than was necessary — for comfort, I told myself. Sometimes my body just does things and my mind has to follow along. That morning, it felt like an elephant was sitting on my chest and I started to cry for no reason at all. Or so I thought. By the time my friends came to the door, I was bawling. And that's when I noticed they'd been crying too. I hugged them hello and saw something like a pop-up image of a car crash behind Sherry's head that I was sure I'd seen the last time I saw her.

And when she told me about her brother's fatal car accident that morning, all that came out of my mouth was, "Oh no, another one?" Of course, I know now that I'd already "seen" what was going to happen and "heard" her tell it very clearly to me, but at the time, it wasn't anything I could understand or face about myself. And when my friends looked confused by what I'd said — because there was only one brother, one fatal accident — I had that all-too-familiar feeling of my cheeks burning up and wanting to sink through the floor. But of course, at that moment, no one cared that what I said seemingly made no sense according to the actual, physical, real-world sequence of events. And I quickly forgot.

Later, I ended up in bed with yet another throbbing migraine — for six days to be exact. When it went away, I forced myself to journal about what happened leading up to the headache attack. I remembered all the little details of what I'll just call a psychic prediction — although maybe there was more to it than that — and when I wrote it down in my headache log, I drew a giant question mark beside it because I didn't know exactly what to do, where to go from there, or why it would have caused me to feel so sick. Looking back, I can see I had so much shame around the things I "knew," that I couldn't quite recognize what was truly there: a long-buried personal treasure.

Eventually I Googled around enough to find out there were psychic schools (thank you, California), so I called one and whispered to the lady on the other end of the phone. I told her I was pretty sure something was wrong, that I needed "protection" from the "negative energy" I was told could make me so sick. And when she laughed sweetly and said words like "empath," "telepath," "medium," and "channel," I started to cry. Soon I was going to secret "meditation classes" a bunch of times a week, and they weren't like the meditation classes I knew at all, but more like playtime with the unseen world.

What followed was the rediscovery of who I truly am, a remembering of once-forgotten gifts I can now see that all humans, plants, animals, and probably even stinkbugs possess: the tools with which to sense formless energies, to discern when they're helpful and when they're not, and the realization that there's nothing we humans don't know about them, nothing we need protection from, other than the totally false belief that we weren't born all-powerful and all-knowing, each with unique superpowers beyond our wildest dreams.

So now I share with you what I've learned on this crazy, funny, wild journey up till now: my stories, some friends' stories, and maybe even a ghost story or two thrown in for good measure. And of course, I've included some of the tools I've found useful for working with the "energies" along the way, in case it may be helpful for you. As my magical, witchy friend Sarah reminded me recently, "Honey, we're never teaching anyone anything — we're just reminding ourselves and maybe some other people about what we already knew." Ugh, too true, sister. Hearing the stories and methods of other people like me was perhaps THE most helpful and empowering thing that happened on my own journey. And so, I give you all this so I might simply remind you (and me) how well we already know all this stuff, how tapped in we already are, how good we are at working with energy. And how we're all a bunch of gifted, talented, all-knowing intuitive psychic channels when we decide to let go of the blocks that have clouded whatever magical genius has been waiting to come through all along. Because if thought creates form (hey, my thoughts created this book), then who wouldn't want to tap into the magic of their own creation?

P.S. This Book Came Through Intuition...

This journey also ended my battle with migraine headaches for good. When a few years ago I woke up with the headache of all headaches, I had a conversation with the pain. I ended up half asleep, in the middle of the night, typing the outline of this thing. And while I'll spare you the details of what definitely won't seem like a normal conversation, I will tell you that by sunrise, I was shiny-faced and smiling, staring at my screen, which had on it something like a how-to and why-the-f*^k-not manual on the subject of everything most of us were never told about the psychic realm. Or reading energy. Or — since we don't have a ton of words in our language yet to describe all of this — what generally falls under the category of "intuition," a word that comes from the Latin *intueri* and refers to a channel. And isn't it so freaking awesome that a book on the subject of intuition came via the mechanism of intuition itself.

How To Use This Book + A Lil' Disclaimer...

In this book, there will be exercises for how to clear blocks, to better read energies and tools that help you access the ways in which you already do (read the energies, that is). You can write directly into the book, save it like a precious little jewel (which would be pretty cool), and for best results, keep a journal of what happens along the way. For additional (and <u>FREE!</u>) resources, please visit my website http://www.courtneyalex.com/book .

This book is in no way, shape, or form meant to tell you what to do. In fact, the whole point of it is to say, hey, do whatever it is you need to do. Which is maybe or maybe not what I need to do too. For now, I write this little disclaimer because I struggled with wanting to share what so very much speaks to my heart, without wanting to project onto you. Because how can a book on intuition be prescriptive? It can't. That feels yucky. So, what follows is just me saying what I know, for now, from my experience with the "unknown" to maybe possibly inspire anyone who happens to read this to simply consider their own experience. I share this as a gift to my own heart, a reminder to walk through its open door, to align with it and follow it always. Enjoy. :)

(fRee Resoyrces!)

Section 1: Getting Clair

Fear vs. Intuition

1.

When Fear Of Intuition Blocks Your Intuition...
(Seriously, That's A Thing)

When I started telling everyone I was writing a book about psychic stuff, energy, and intuition...well, I didn't. I got so many weird looks and blank stares that after a while, I started sharing only with a handful of friends I knew would understand. And even those who could relate to my more interesting energetic experiences expressed concerns like "What if your book falls into the wrong hands?" Seriously, that was a question. Or "What if my intuition is already so good, my sensitivity so strong, that if I work on it anymore, I'm going to know every single thing about every single person I see?" Probably a waste of time. And then there were questions like "Can you see what I'm thinking right now?", "What if it goes against my religion?" and "What if I get so caught up in the spirit world, I end up floating away or taking on "bad" energy or getting sick or seeing that someone's going to die or become possessed by ghosts and all that?" Or perhaps the biggest question many of us are secretly struggling with: "What if my intuition just hasn't worked like it's supposed to? What if my logical mind is at odds with my intuitive one? What if I do this intuition thing...wrong?"

While some of these questions may sound familiar or otherwise totally ridiculous to you, the fact is they're all rooted in fear. And fear is a nasty culprit that blocks intuition — even more so, when the thing that's got you afraid is using intuition itself. If you've got some funny beliefs about what is scary (and we all do), your survival instincts push those things away — even if, on some level, they're things you want. Like having my intuition tell me to write a book about intuition, while at the same time, being totally scared to talk to people about intuition. See? As humans, we have a lot of unconscious and often silly-sounding fears. And you know what? I've since started talking a lot about energy, and I'm still breathing.

But I've learned, from my chats with people on the topic, that some of you are having trouble with this stuff — either experiencing so much energetic or intuitive sensitivity to the point you can't leave the house (been there) or questioning how or why to trust your intuition at all (been there too). Since we tend to be scared of what we don't know, and this stuff went un-talked about for way too long, many of us are, on some level, afraid.

Fear Vs. Intuition

So first things first, let's work on clearing up fear, as it's one of the biggest blocks to intuition. Let's talk about some of the reasons you think you may *not* want to be a super psychic intuitive channel, reading energy all the time, so that for the rest of the book, we can work on building trust and belief in doing just that.

A question I'm often asked is, "What's the difference between fear and intuition?" Many of us can't tell. And hey, it's a complex question. Gut-based intuition has to do with physical survival, and so will often have a large say in the choices we make about our needs. It's meant to tell us when our safety's at stake. And so, beliefs related to survival needs like food, shelter, money, even sex — hey, the survival of our human race depends on it — will often drive our gut-based decisions, which means the beliefs we have around survival will drive our gut-based decisions. So, even if a seemingly silly fear, like *What if I use my intuition wrong?* isn't a real threat to your body (at least not most of the time), the gut might perceive that it is.

When we feel fear, our bodies contract, blocking the flow of energy and our inner communication pathways along with it. Throw in the logical mind that wants to solve everything based on the past, and some stories and beliefs we've been told, and you've got something of an intuitive gridlock. When this happens, the only message that comes through is "Warning." Think of something you're afraid of right now, and feel your body clam up. Are you feeling in the flow? I don't think so. Now, switch to the thought of something you love and let's move on.

Let's talk about third eye, heart, and gut. We all have different energy centers, different places from which to sense and make intuitive decisions, and these are three major ones. And if your heart wants one thing, but your gut thinks it's a threat, you might feel like you're at odds with yourself. Relationships are a great example of this. Have you ever had your heart broken? Do you sometimes act in funny ways when it comes to love and connection? Does one part of you try to be close to someone, while another part pushes them away? Or do you know someone who does this? Right. If your gut intuition says you were so heartbroken the last time it felt this energy pattern from your heart that you couldn't eat, it will steer you away from what it perceives as a real survival threat. Or what about this one: Does your gut ever tell you that you don't have time to do what you really love because you need to make money doing something else, even though you know you'd be better at the thing you love, and you already have enough stuff? See how fear can get the best of your intuition? How it can even create the illusion that your gut's intuition is steering you toward a real need, or even cause unnecessary worry, anxiety or stress?

So, how do you work with this? By facing the fears you may not even know you have. By clearing your energetic and intuitive pathways — so that your third eye connects to your heart and connects to your gut — and learning to hear the messages from your inner self. By understanding how your intuition communicates through subtle energetic sound bites. We'll get to all of that in this book. Because when you know so well how to listen in, you can do it more regularly, with so much ease. And last, by transforming old fear patterns into something more useful — like wisdom — you can shed light on the things you've been in the dark about for way too long. So let's get started transforming some fear, shall we?

Exercise: *Transforming Fear*

Before we get into the fun stuff, let's make room by clearing away what is way un-fun. By talking about our fears, we transform their energy to that of understanding, extract their gems of wisdom that can help us on our path. It's like dumping onto the table what felt like yucky mystery sand from the bottom of your bag only to discover there was something precious in there you really needed. Are you ready? I'm ready. And if you're seriously ready, you might as well just say YES out loud. Because using your voice, creating vibration, is a powerful way to move and break up old patterns of energy you don't want or need.

So, here are some reasons why I have, at times, been afraid of my own sensitive nature, my gift for intuition. These happen to be reasons why I have mumbled at times when telling people I'm a psychic, medium, intuitive, energy worker, sensory human...or whatever we're going to call this. But that's over now. I list this stuff here so you can then do the same, and then get inspired to come up with some of your own. Then we'll let it go to the Earth to be transformed, composted, and turned into something more useful for the good of all beings everywhere. Here goes...

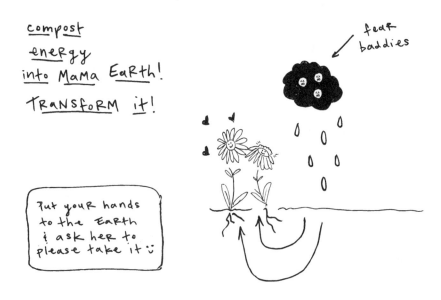

8 Reasons I Used To Be Afraid
To Talk About Psychic & Intuitive Stuff

1. **Because it's embarrassing to meet a cute guy or a friend's boss at a party and tell them I'm an intuitive who wrote a wildly successful book on psychic stuff and watch them lean back and look away so I can't read what they're thinking.**

Maybe I opened with the most ridiculous one. But it's real, so I wrote it. And it's probably one of the reasons I'm so fired up to explain more about the energies. Please know that since time and space don't totally limit this line of work, I could be reading your mind right now. And if that's the case, backing away from this page won't change a thing. BUT since poring over the fine details of everyone I meet is exhausting — and frankly, I'd rather focus on my own day — I'm not out to read anyone's mental diary or steal anyone's bank card info just for fun. And if I were, I'd seriously have to question my intentions. Basically, I only do this stuff when asked. So, I set this one free. (And if you're sensitive like me and prone to hearing everyone's mind chatter, read on, friends. I have some tips that will quiet down the noise.)

2. **My family who believes very much in science and math will refer to me as the weird one.**

Too late. But they love me as I am and know I'm awesome and smart and definitely the kind of chica who used to get an "A" in calculus class anyway, so I set this free. Logic + intuition = one powerful combo. It's right and left brain working together, it's intuition giving us the theory part of the all-important math or science experiment. We've got to have a hunch about something before we can prove it to be true. The left hand washes the right, opposites attract, two heads are better than one, and so on — you get it. Many great inventions of our time were born of these two friends coming together. I love and honor and can't wait to share even more about my intuitive psychic and even logic-loving self.

3. Everyone in the world is technically all-knowing and because of that, they already know everything I think I know, and they probably even know it better.

What? I know. But oooooh, this was a big one for me, as a claircognizant, a person who gets "downloads" of information but was told by my culture that I cannot possibly know things I haven't been directly told. I have a sore spot around what I know and what I don't, what to speak up about. And yet, while it is true that all of us can do this in some capacity — we all already know all the things that are true for us — many of us have simply stuffed it down or forgot or blocked it. Or worse, we have doubted ourselves. We have told ourselves we can't. So, in this case, hearing the stories and methods of others like me — that is, other humans who know so much of their own truth but never gave themselves permission to embrace it — was perhaps THE most helpful, empowering, and validating thing that happened on my own journey, so I set that freaking free and cannot wait to share more.

4. But seriously, what if I'm wrong?

Yup, again, this is a wound I'm still licking. Ever read the myth of Cassandra? The woman who was cursed with knowing everything, yet no one would believe her? Even though she's totally right about everything? I'm not saying I'm right about everything, per se, but like I said, there was a point in time where downloading "knowings" made life confusing. Especially when others denied what I said. A basic but great example: "Are you mad at me?" You ask your friend because you sense she's mad at you. She says, "No, what are you talking about?" Even though she is. Situations as small as these certainly led to my questioning whether I could trust myself. Or anyone, for that matter. We'll get into more of that soon, since self-trust is a big block to intuition for many, especially those who are gifted at it.

So many times in my life, I was confused as to whether I was just imagining knowing things, and there were times my knowings weren't confirmed until years later. So the point is...I no longer care if I could be wrong. I now trust myself completely. Since everyone's interpretation of truth is their own anyway, and I claim to know no more or less than what has been my own life experience…I. Set. It. Free. I do my best to see love in everything and trust in the higher order of things. None of us are all-knowingly perfect, otherwise this Earth School wouldn't be any fun, right? What makes for the easiest flow of intuition? Surrendering to the right to be wrong. Seriously. That means allowing ourselves to make mistakes and trusting that if we mess up the instructions, there must be a perfect reason for it.

5. What if people think I'm crazy, or what if I actually go crazy?

Too late. But I love my own brand of crazy. But maybe you once heard a story about a friend of a friend who got into this stuff and went bonkers. And so I ask: Did it happen to you? No? Okay. So where do these random warnings come from? It wasn't long ago that famed American mystic and Bible-lover Edgar Cayce was jailed for practicing and talking about this stuff — and let's not even get into witch burning. There's a lot of societal "stuff" here. But if we all promise not to creep out others by saying things like, "The reason I was late and didn't text was because my spirit guide Heyzar…" I think we'll be just fine. Let's be discerning, grounded, joyous, and connected to our Earthly reality and…set this one free. We will cover grounding, which will keep us from floating off into the ethers and is crucial to understanding how to use our "downloads" in daily life. It will also help us love and embrace our own beautiful crazy in a healthy and useful way.

6. What if I "see" something I'd rather not?

This used to be a big thing for me as a sensitive person, before I realized that whatever information comes must be useful for some purpose, even if it's just a reminder to focus on something un-scary! We choose what we see, we choose what to focus on, always. I know that if I focus on love, if I focus on fun, if I focus on the bright side, I will see things that way. We are free and safe, especially if we've got sharp intuition. I let my limiting beliefs go and set that one free.

7. What if I take on "bad" energy?

See #6. This feels BIG and SCARY if you're sensitive. I know it. But the thing is, since we always have choice, we're the ones who decide to engage with a specific pattern of energy. I'll expand on that in a bit. For now, I'll say I believe there is no such thing as this, especially wherever there's joy and laughter. All lessons in life are here to help bring us closer to love, if we're open to seeing it that way. I am. And by the way, like attracts like in energy, so if you spot it, you've also got it, my friend!

8. What if people think I'm blaspheming God or an established religion, spiritual tradition, or faith?

Well I did have Bible quotes to support this, but I didn't want to leave any one religion out so I ditched 'em. The thing is: When you pray, in any language, faith or tradition, you're using the tools of intuition, because you're speaking to a higher — and usually formless — power greater than yourself. And if you're atheist, maybe you're even consulting a wiser all-knowing version of yourself sometimes. In any case, I have the utmost respect and reverence for the higher order; I am simply in awe. And therefore free.

NOW...8 of Your Own!

Now is when to ask you to list eight of your own fears. Because the more you let go of fear — and doesn't it sound silly when we get it all out? — the more space opens up for intuitive insight to flow in. One of my favorite clients recently asked me, "What if I try one of your intuitive exercises and I do it wrong?" If this is one of your fears, please list it so you can ditch it. Using your intuition fully means doing things your way, which may not be the same way as others. And by the way, your fears don't have to be related to intuition for it to be powerfully transformative when you let them go. If you can't think of any just now, try closing your eyes, getting really quiet, and asking to be "shown" your fears. Not only does this work well, but it's a good way to start flexing your intuitive skill!

8 of Your Super Scary
(But Possibly Also Silly-Sounding) Fears

1. _____

2. _____

3. _____

4. _____

5. _____

6. _____

7. _____

8. _____

Shedding Light On Fear

So, let's expand on some of this stuff now, because there are definitely some themes here that tend to come up again and again. First up:

Fear Of Being Wrong

"What if I try to follow my intuition, but I don't do it right?" This is a heady question. Because if you think about it, if you've done an intuitive exercise the way your body directed you to, then you were technically following your intuition. And it's true, there are tried and tested methods for a lot of this stuff, but learning via intuition — if intuition refers to a hunch that logic can later test out — means learning from experience. And for that to happen, we've got to experience everything, whether it be "right" or "wrong." I'll refer to the ancient Chinese model of energy, which teaches about yin and yang. The point of that cute little circle symbol is not to show us that everything is black and white, but that together they make up a whole picture, which means, both sides are equally important. Being right is just as relevant as being wrong. And anyway, if we stand to learn from our mistakes, is there such a thing as making one?

The real problem comes when we decide not to learn from our experiences, to cut off the emotional or energetic flow we feel during and after them. If you analyze rather than feel the depth of an experience, it's possible you'll end up in the same pattern again and again. Our spirit wants to grow, to learn. Someone once said you never get second chances in life, but all I see are second chances... and thirds...and fourths...I'm just a tiny human, but from where I stand, it certainly seems like our spirits provide us with the same situations over and over again, until we've truly felt the energy of them, learned our lessons fully, extracted their wisdom, surrendered to any fear, to the "danger" of being wrong. Are you working with the same type of boss all the time? Dating the same type of girl or guy? See? Second chances everywhere. Be open to being wrong about the outcome, to feeling fully what that feels like, and you may just transform the experience, the energy of it, altogether.

What if you're afraid you're wrong about the very existence of this energy stuff? Of your own experiences with it? Well, this is a biggie for most of us in the West because our culture has not taught us much about energy. So, sometimes our experiences with the "unseen" world does make us question whether we can trust ourselves. For now, just know there are many out there like you. We'll work on self-trust in Chapter 2.

Fear Of Needing To "Protect" Ourselves

There's an old saying: "Where the mind goes, energy flows." The second you choose to focus on protecting yourself, you're likely going to attract something you need protection from. Like attracts like in energy, so the best "defense" is to simply focus on what you want to attract. I like to say that rather than hold up a metaphoric shield around your space — which gets heavy and draining after a while — why not fill your space up with all that you love, thereby leaving no room for what you don't?

And what if you believe in bad juju? Even if just a little bit? When we judge "good" or "bad," the things we label as "bad" are generally what we feel we need protection from. This applies to the more mysterious variety of beings from the spirit world we've learned about from scary movies to even the little things. Perhaps it's a belief system or pattern that doesn't align with what your intuitive sense is telling you, and you're making yourself feel bad as a result. Here's a good example of this is: All dessert is bad for me. Sure, if I believe the chocolate I'm eating is making me fat or sick, then I will feel bad about myself, and I'll technically be eating the vibes of shame and guilt. But if I decide I love it, that it makes my heart happy (and it does), then I'll feel good after I eat it instead. This is why praying before our food or making Reiki hands over it works so well: we're fusing what we take into our bodies with the energy of what we want to experience.

And while it's my belief that in energy there is no "good" or '"bad" — although I've used those words a lot — we still want to do right by other humans, so it's ideal to check our perceptions, intentions, and how we feel and act around certain people, places, and spaces. And that's why I like to refer to "bad" vibes as belief systems or behavior patterns that can keep us feeling stuck, heavy, small, or in victim mode. And sure, these patterns can feel big and scary, hard to shake, but that's because they're often patterns many people believe in, or maybe they've been passed down by our family, friends, or culture at large, even though we don't believe in them at our very core. And this sometimes causes anxiety, a misalignment with our intuition, the confused feeling of being at odds with ourselves. Nonetheless, we can choose to shift what we believe, and that changes our experience.

Our external world always mirrors what we've got going on inside, our ideas. So if you feel you're attracting some energy pattern you want protection from — like sickness every time you eat dessert due to guilt or shame, or something of the heavier variety — just notice your words, your beliefs, and ask, "Do I want this as part of my experience?" And if not, "What would I rather have instead?"

Fear Of Being Too Energetically Sensitive

I'm going to say it again: Where the mind goes, energy flows. When we've been super attuned to reading others and our surroundings, then we will continue to do so until we make a conscious effort not to. So, if you tend to pick up on other people's energy more easily than your own, the trick is to focus on your own energy more often, which we'll be doing in a lot of different ways in the coming chapters.

Often, when we're perceiving too much, it's actually a direct result of fear. Many of us who grew up being fed fear beliefs, in dangerous cities or situations, with trauma, or with parents or ancestors who came from trauma as mine did, are hyper-tuned to sensing our surroundings — and this is actually based on fear beliefs and patterns we were taught about the constant need to look for safety. Energetically, for me, this looked like my radar was spread out super far so that I could sense what was down an alleyway two miles away. This is useful when there's the threat of actual danger in that alleyway, but when there's not, it's just distracting. It's like having 100 radio antennas all picking up different sounds and signals.

Also, because of the survival patterns I'd gotten used to, sometimes I'd leave my body altogether, which would leave my space open to picking up on all kinds of energy without my directing the intention toward what I wanted to feel and sense. Many people have come to my workshops curious to know more about these "out of body" experiences. But you know what's even more interesting and fun? An *inner* body experience. Take up your own energetic space, and your intuitive capacities (along with your unique magical gifts) will be strengthened in a big way.

For we empaths and healers who might've grown up with the belief that it was our job to solve all the problems in our families, protecting ourselves from "bad" vibes may mean being extra cautious in not trying to fix everyone we meet. It's a big no-no to "take on" someone else's lessons, to offer help when it's not requested — because then others can't learn for themselves. When we try to help everyone, we're actually making things worse for others and for ourselves. And maybe you're not actively giving advice, but you are worried about whether another person's going to be okay? When you do that, you're not only giving your focus and therefore your energy to that person, but you're also sending a message that says, "I don't trust you can do this on your own." And that is not support.

Since we all sense energy, other people will feel it and want to push your worry vibes away. And that's what feels draining — the entire pattern, not the other person's energy. If this seems hard to shift, it isn't. What's one easy way to do this? Simply direct your juicy love and healing energy elsewhere — for instance, at yourself. Because you were only given one body to control, and therefore you're the only person you can ever truly heal. Compassion and love for ourselves emanates outward. As we get to reading our own energy, it will be easy to see where the leaks are.

And what about energy-hungry vampires? You may not be familiar with this term, but it has been written about and it's yet another way we tend to believe we're victim to "bad" vibes. The term "vampire" has been used to refer to those people who literally want to suck your life-blood. We've all met these people — yes, they exist — and God bless the fact we're all born with our own special roles to play in this world. While it may seem like these people are a threat to our energetic space, this is really just another case of making choices, of asking ourselves where we're directing our energy and why. Because when someone's in our energetic space or drawing on our energy, it's only because we've chosen to open up space to them, to offer up a taste of our delicious energy. After all, a vampire doesn't come in unless you invite me. Hehe.

Fear Of Perceiving Too Much

What if you think you're too sensitive? Then congratulations because you are also super gifted at working with energy and being intuitive. Chances are, you might have played it down a bit over the years, even if unconsciously, because you heard one too many times something like, "Stop being so sensitive." And on some level, you tried. And on another, it hurt. But most importantly, it probably only worked a little and with varying degrees of success, mostly to confuse you about what your intuition and energy channels even felt like or were trying to tell you. And I also have to assume that you, like me, also heard too many times, "Oh, you're just too sensitive." And you might've even believed there is such a thing. But if that's your nature, it's pretty much like someone telling you you're being too much of yourself. Which really hurts. And I know it. I once tried to be a little less of myself too and let me tell you — this way feels much better.

The word "sensitivity" has, in the Western world, somehow been equated with weakness, a trait we've felt the need to overcome. But being a sensitive person means being someone who's strong at sensing, which means we're good at picking up subtle cues that less sensitive people may not. In the animal kingdom, we can look to the deer, who represents sensitivity itself, and in many traditions, is revered for her ability to sense danger before any other animal in the forest. She is therefore indispensable to her fellow fauna. And that, my dear sensitive sisters and brothers, is powerful — not to mention useful to the community as a whole. In modern human terms, it means we're good with trends and creativity, we're conscientious and kind because we can feel into people, places, and spaces. It all comes easily via intuition, so much so that it may not even seem like much. But it is if we open up to it, release the fear associated with it, and allow it to flow.

What if you struggle with being an empath, someone who feels the feelings of others, sometimes stronger than your own? I once struggled with this, only to find out the feelings *were* my own. Other people were simply triggering me to stop burying the emotions I hadn't wanted to feel for so long, as a result of being afraid to be so sensitive. Sometimes we tend to be empathic when we've got stagnant energy built up in the emotional layer of the subtle body.

The good news is that because we empaths are gifted at feeling into the depths of our energetic layers, we're good at working with them too. Deepening intuition is something that's really easy for us, as is releasing old stagnant energy we no longer need. And learning to read energy in a conscious way helped me to recognize what I was picking up, and to choose when it was helpful to do so. So I say all you have to do is love your beautiful empath self and strengthen your energetic sensitivity by understanding it, and the struggle part falls away.

What about when external vibes seem to be causing actual physical pain? Usually it's not the person, place, or thing that's causing it, but your reaction to it. Are you scared of taking on vibes? Then it's your fear of taking on the vibes that could be causing the problem. In fact, you can even classify *that* as using your intuition — in a sense that it's trying to show you what sort of fears are not serving you so you can learn and grow. Understanding how to work with energy and intuition can help rid us of the type of fear that manifests as physical pain. How cool is that?

Kasia & The Legs

My friend Kasia used to tell me she couldn't be in a room with her coworker Jason. She dreaded weekly meetings with him, where she'd feel sluggish, heavy, and drained. Eventually, it got so bad, her legs went numb whenever she was in the conference room with him, until one day, she landed in the hospital because of it. When we talked about her problem, she'd beat herself up. "I guess I'm just too sensitive," she said. "I just can't deal with Jason or his energy."

Now it's true that Jason was a pain to be around. Whenever I met him outside of office hours, I usually found myself walking away. He was a super interrupter, a guy that needed all eyes on him all the time. Having a conversation with him was like watching a movie or talking to a wall. When he did hear something you said, it didn't matter, because you were never right unless you were agreeing with him. Worse, if you did try to offer a different take on something, he'd throw a fit like a toddler who just lost his favorite toy. And so, if you knew the guy, you knew it was best to just smile, nod and walk away.

Kasia, on the other hand, is a mama type. She's not happy unless everyone else is happy, unless the whole room is feeling the love. She's the type of friend who would come to your art opening even if it's two hours away and she's been sick in bed all day; she'll spend all day texting friends to make sure they know they're loved. So of course, she gave that same treatment to Jason, and he responded by being even more of a steamroller to her, interrupting her every chance he could get. The rest of us wondered how she could stand it. But when she was around him, literally, she could not stand.

So here's the question: Was Kasia feeling sick because of the energy Jason was throwing her way, or because she was lying to herself about her own? Let's come back to this story in a sec...

Subtle Energy Science, Genetic 1's & 0's

When developmental biologist Bruce Lipton was in grad school studying stem cell clones, he observed an interesting effect. His samples, identical muscle tissue cells mostly, behaved differently depending on where they were left overnight. In other words, he noticed that single cells, just like humans, were sensing and reacting to their environment.

In his best-selling book, *The Biology of Belief*, he offers an explanation. In it, he looks to a single-celled organism called a prokaryote. With not much more than a nucleus, cytoplasm, and a membrane, the prokaryote seems to move toward or away from whatever's close by that is either beneficial or harmful to its survival. It does this by expanding or contracting. What's more interesting is that even without its nucleus (the part commonly thought of as the cell's brain), it does the same thing.

How does it know what's beneficial or harmful to its survival? According to Dr. Lipton and now several other biologists, the answer may be linked to its membrane — the skin of the cell, or outermost layer — and its ability to perceive. Which is cool, because this sounds pretty similar to our own body of energy. And apparently, a human stem cell reacts the same way. If our cell receptor senses something beneficial to its survival, it will move toward that external stimulus, thereby expanding.

On the other hand, if the stimulus seems to pose a threat to survival, the cell will contract or move away. It's kind of like genetic binary code, producing either a 1 or 0 answer to the question "Is this good for me?" And as Lipton so eloquently states, cells will not just respond to chemical stimuli but also to certain emotion, beliefs, and thoughts — in other words, energy. So, if our bodies are made up of trillions of stem cells, all responding to external stimuli, wouldn't it make sense that Kasia's cells, and therefore her legs, would contract in order to tell her something too?

AND...Now Back To Kasia & The Legs

So now back to the story. I ask, Why would Kasia's legs and her trillions of tiny leg cells contract if Jason wasn't truly a threat to Kasia's survival? Yes, he was definitely a threat to any enjoyable conversation, but it's not like he was going to actually hurt anybody. And yet, even as Kasia talked about the guy, she was like a deer in headlights, tripping over her words. Her fear of him, even the idea of him, was very real to her. And while it's true that Jason himself wasn't dangerous, Kasia's inability to speak up for herself and be discerning about who she gave love to definitely was. That's where the true fear was to be found, the energy block, the generator of such a "bad vibe."

You might be asking, Why just her legs? Why wouldn't her whole body contract in the face of potential danger? Well, there are a few possible explanations — it's the reason why our intuition isn't always totally clear, and we'll get into that in the next chapters. Regardless of why, the beauty of it was when Kasia finally realized that any time her legs went numb in that way, it was a signal she'd better speak up more clearly. So in that sense, it was not her sensitivity working against her, but it was an attempt for her body to communicate an issue, a totally solvable one, that needed her attention. And in the end, it did. Her once frustrating pain became her best friend.

While Jason's still difficult — after all, you can't change another person — Kasia chose to face her fear of not being heard, and so her reaction to him subsided completely and she hasn't been to the hospital since. In fact, now when her legs start to squeeze, she goes outside and takes a break to collect herself, comes back in and speaks up.

self-trust

2.

Sally Eats Lunch In The Alley

My friend Sally is a fellow psychic sister, an empath who used to have a penchant for punishment. Well, not consciously anyway. But she had a thing for dating men who seemed to feed off her beautiful energy. Maybe on some level she wanted to save them, or maybe she'd simply gotten used to these types of relationships. Regardless, she was breaking up with one when she enrolled in a woodworking class and instantly attracted another. Let's call him Charles.

Charles was gorgeous and he knew it. When the teacher began class by explaining the project for the day, Charles would position himself somewhere behind the teacher, take his top off and let down his long blonde hair. You couldn't help but not look at Charles as he tossed his hair and danced his hips around. Like most of the class, Sally would be totally distracted by the end of the demo, tired, drained of energy, and weirdly, Charles often seemed to be flashing his dimples at her. She tried her best to look away and keep her energy to herself. He asked her to be his woodworking partner. Normally, she'd find this endearing — flattering, even — but since she had a pattern of choosing men who'd eventually use her energy in unhelpful ways — like for borrowing money and never paying it back — she was playing it safe.

At the time, she was also learning to read energy, studying the dynamics of voice. "When he first told me his name," she said, "something sounded not right. His voice was pinched, like he was holding something back." When she took some distance, he'd follow her around the wood shop, stand by the door when she wanted to go outside for break, and when she spoke to him, she found herself instinctively holding back, not sharing much about herself at all. And when he still wouldn't quit following her around, she took lunch solo, eating in the alleyway beside the studio where she couldn't easily be found. She was usually pretty social. "I don't know, Court, it just felt right to be far away from him," she told me. Eventually, Charles disappeared and stopped coming to class altogether. And when that happened, she naturally rejoined the group.

Once he was totally out of the picture, she asked another student what happened to Charles. "He got arrested," said the classmate. "Turns out Charles wasn't even his real name!" Apparently, he'd been wanted in the state of Iowa, but nobody knew why. And thanks to Sally's newfound trust of her own spidey-senses, she never had to find out.

How do you know you are probably a naturally gifted psychic intuitive channeling reader of energy? If you have ever seriously betrayed yourself like Sally used to, that's how. And I say that because I have struggled so much with this that I figure it must be for some good reason — or at least that's what I like to tell myself. But it makes sense, because how do you develop a strong sense of intuition? An unwavering sense of self-trust? Well, one way is to learn what the opposite feels like. Study every single facet of trust and mistrust, honesty and betrayal until you have absolutely no doubt what it means to have full faith. And beyond that, to trust that every situation you've ever found yourself in — yes, even the ones that make you want to crawl into a hole — has taught some type of helpful lesson, even more about the topic of trust. And I often wonder if having a strong sense of self-trust and good intuition are one and the same. It's my hope to share some of the less painful ways of building self-trust, to help you repair it if it's been broken.

On Self-Trust

Another big block to having clear intuition is our sense of self-trust. Because let's face it, why would you want to listen to a voice that's seemingly steered you wrong in the past? To one you may not know much about? A voice that stays quiet and doesn't seem to make clear decisions at times? Or one you think you might even be making up? Over the course of our lives, we have all questioned our choices. And no doubt, we've all made mistakes — or at least it's felt like we have, since life lessons are not always comfy, especially not the big ones. And while pain is the touchstone of growth, some of us might have chosen to learn lessons in super un-fun ways over very long periods of time. After all, life is hard, right? Actually, no. It doesn't have to be. And neither does it have to be to better trust your inner voice. So what does all the trust stuff boil down to? Well, trust in anything comes from self-trust, and there are a few good ways to get there.

Honesty

Honesty is perhaps the most important part of developing a keen sense of intuition. While you can never control or truly understand the motivation of others, you can always work to better know yourself. The more honest you are with yourself, about your needs, your intentions, your loves and limitations — especially the patterns and habits you don't enjoy — the more in sync you get with your inner voice.

Now, I'm sorry, but being honest with yourself does not mean justifying your actions when you're lost or seemingly messing up. Trying to tell yourself you have answers when you don't or trying to make yourself look better — even if only to yourself — is similar to dishonesty. And, hey, it happens, but lying to yourself blocks you from hearing your inner voice because...well, for one thing, How well do you trust people who've lied to you? Right. So, tell yourself the truth, for better or worse, no matter how ugly or shameful or beautifully misunderstood you may be, as step #1 for rebuilding self-trust. And by the way, there's plenty of room for error here, so long as you can be honest when you think you might've made a mistake, so long as you're willing to apologize...to yourself.

The more you're willing to listen to your honest truth, the more your inner voice feels heard, and therefore the more confident it feels to speak up and be heard. And in that sense, when you give your inner voice the respect and honor it deserves, it thrives. This allows room for mistakes, for being human and learning from experience, which translates to more free-flowing energy, allowing your energetic (and intuitive) pathways to open. Being at odds with ourselves causes our bodies to contract and self-protect, while being truthful means feeling like we have more room to open up and be ourselves. Contraction constricts your energy flow and therefore your flow of inner communication signals. Expansion, on the other hand, allows those signals to get where they need to go, which translates to being able to quickly perceive and act on your intuitive guidance. So, in order to build trust, honor the real and even ugly truth, rather than trying to hide parts of yourself away.

Being honest with ourselves also means we'll have better boundaries. Over time, you'll find yourself automatically speaking up for or acting on your needs without having to think twice. Sally did it, for instance, when she ate lunch by herself, automatically removing herself from a situation that would've caused her trouble in the past. And it worked both ways, because once she was honest about what she perceived in herself — that she had a tendency to attract men who might take advantage of her, and on some level, she was choosing to be taken advantage of — she got useful information about the situation she was in and what to do. So, honesty around perceptions of yourself begets honesty around perceptions of the world too, which allows you to shift your experience with both. We'll get deeper into this as we get to reading our own energy — it's so useful!

The more trustworthy you are with yourself, the more you attract trustworthy people into your sphere because like attracts like in energy. When you're honest, it inspires others and gives them permission and space to do the same. So, even if you don't fully trust yourself yet, but you can get honest, you'll have more people coming around to show you examples of honesty and trust in the external world. Eventually, this translates to trust in your inner world too. It's really pretty cool. So let's exercise this part of ourselves, shall we?

Exercise: **Tapping Into Honesty**

Write down one thing you'd rather others didn't know. Maybe it's something you feel you've done "wrong," maybe you needed to do it, or you knew that what you were doing would get you in trouble somehow and you did it anyway. No justifications, please. In fact, the harder it is to admit, the better it'll feel once you do. And if you're having trouble with this, you can practice some self-trust right now by just allowing the first thing that comes to mind to flow out of your pen or your mouth, never to be spoken of again. Up to you. I trust you ;)

_____
_____
_____
_____
_____

And if you need a buddy in this, here's one of mine: I used to dumb myself down around people because I was taught that a wise woman is also an unpopular one, so I purposely made myself sound stupid or acted small because I wanted to be liked. Oooh, does that sound gross to me now, but it feels so good to get it off my chest.

Surrender

Seriously, I hated this word until I typed it just now. Because while I know it works, I'm definitely not someone who likes to surrender my will, especially if I don't have a good reason for doing so. And when I'm in a state where surrender is the only option, when I'm really feeling bad or mad or stuck? Ooof. Well, it's kind of like having someone tell me to "just relax" exactly at the moment I'm about to lose my s^*t completely. Those are the words that can actually make me lose my s^*t, now that I think about it. Or at least this is what the words, "Hey, just surrender, babe," did for me until I found a super easy way to do it.

Over time, I have found that true surrender simply means being honest with myself about the fact that I have no answer. It means giving up the will to try and control what I don't yet understand. That is the stuff I tend to feel hopeless and helpless about — because how can you get the right answer when you can't even come up with the right question to ask? How can you find yourself if you don't know for certain you are lost? Or don't want to admit it? You can't. You simply cannot follow your GPS to where you want to go unless you have the exact location of where you happen to be. And on that note, you probably won't pull out your phone to check for directions until you can admit to yourself that you don't know your way.

So, in that regard, surrender means admitting first that you are lost, maybe feeling like you need help, unable to understand what you want or need, unsure of how to find it...but that's the sweet spot actually, because at least you do know that you are in surrender-ville. And it's in this super quiet, honest, empty and receptive spot that our intuition has no choice but to kick in. This is the space where answers somehow, as if by magic, just come.

If you're in this space right now and it doesn't seem to be working, try saying these words out loud: "I feel hopeless and helpless here and I don't know what I want or need." Because, hey — you never know who (or what) is listening. Even better, speak out loud what it is you feel hopeless or helpless about. The more shameful or guilt-provoking it feels to say it, the better it usually feels once it's out of your mouth.

Are you not quitting a job you hate because deep down you believe you can never find one you'd love? Are you staying in a destructive relationship, telling yourself it's fine, because you're afraid you won't get a nicer date? Are you not spending money because you think making money is hard and doesn't come to people like you? Well, you're not alone. I wouldn't be writing these things if I didn't once believe them too. But do you know how good it feels to admit it all? Light, and a little like magic.

So how does one surrender in the most efficient way possible? Again, it's easy: When you're at the point of considering the idea of digging a hole in the forest and bringing a whole pile of snacks with you if only you had the will to do it...just admit it. Honesty with yourself improves your intuition by bringing forth your own unique truth. To surrender is to ask an open question and welcome answers.

Exercise: In Surrender

Next time you feel stuck and really don't want to surrender, just admit it. Even admit to feeling stuck, helpless, or hopeless. Do nothing else. Don't push it. A few days later, think back to what happened, what emotions and thoughts came, and do a lil' journal if you feel like it.

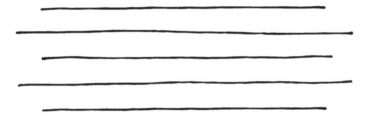

Trusting Past Mistakes

So, I already talked about the importance of being wrong, of learning through experience, but let's talk about the fact there is a totally false belief that those who have a strong sense of intuition will have perfect lives. No way. I have made some big-time mistakes in my life, and like I said, I'm pretty sure I had to make them in order to sharpen my intuition. Having a keen sense simply means trusting that every experience we choose is for good reason. And after a while, you know what? It gets easier to see what those reasons are.

A wise teacher of mine once said that we must learn through our three intuitive centers in order to truly know something. She pointed to the third eye, heart, and gut, and gave this example: Let's say you see someone riding a bike, and want to learn...well, at that point, you might know about riding a bike, might've even read the manual, but probably can't do it expertly yet. And for the sake of this book, let's say your intuition led you to the street where someone happened to be riding a cool-looking bike that made you want to learn.

Anyway, after you saw the bike riding happen, your passion, your heart's intuition might lead you to actually get on a bike. At this point, you can feel the sensation of getting on one, the excitement of when you finally get up or fall. And at that point, you might be familiar with riding a bike, but you're still not an expert. Eventually, you ride some more and your body gets the rhythm, and you know how to ride a bike, even when you haven't done it for years. The whole messy but fun process is what it really means to know, deep in your core. In other words, for strong intuition, you also need strong experience.

To build trust, you need to know what it feels like to waver at it too. So, making mistakes, truly knowing what those mistakes feel like in your body and not just as a concept in your mind, is crucial. And while I'd love to provide a safe and easy-feeling exercise for doing this...well, I'm sorry, friends, but the point I'm trying to make is, this is life. And the exercise I'd give would simply tell you to go out and live. And trust in those times you took a spill while learning.

Again, having strong intuition doesn't mean you won't make mistakes, and it doesn't mean you won't learn lessons — you will — but when you trust your actions fully, you let go of focusing on them so you can move on and have new and different experiences. And this means not having to repeat lessons — because where the mind goes, energy flows, and sometimes our feet follow that track too. Basically, don't focus energy on what you don't want to happen. It's like letting go of thoughts about when you fell off the bike, while choosing to focus instead on the fact you're now better at riding.

Accepting and even loving your past "mistakes" is conveniently akin to self-forgiveness: It energetically releases these patterns from your field, which keeps you from making the same intuitive choices you'd rather not. It's like if you've had a tendency to lend money to people who never pay you back, would you want to go around bragging about it, making yourself into an easy target for more people to do the same? Or would you let it go, stop talking about it, and decide you're good with that experience and would rather not mess with that energy again? Whatever you think about, you bring near. And what if you can't stop thinking about something or keep getting involved in the same pattern? Your intuition probably knows you've still got some lessons to learn. So…trust it. It may not be a mistake after all.

Trusting in past mistakes is trusting in ourselves and in the great order of things. This doesn't mean brushing off the tough stuff as if it were nothing, excusing poor behavior from others, declaring that none of it matters anymore and you're totally unfazed. That's not realistic, especially if the stakes are high. All it takes is saying to yourself, Okay, I kinda see why that needed to happen. I sorta see what I learned, or at least I'm open to the fact I might be still learning something, even if I don't know what it is yet. Because our intuition often chooses a path that gives us what we need, rather than what we think we want. And if you're at least open to admit that, the energy around it eases up; a path that wasn't previously available suddenly makes itself known. And if you still need a push, just consider this: The only way to change the past is to change your present and future attitude about it. For now, anyway. So why not try this out, and see how much weight it carries?

Exercise: Trust Your Past Mistakes

Think of a mistake you feel you've made. Really feel it in your body. Now declare out loud simply that you're learning from it, maybe even what you're learning from it, if you already know. Now feel that one in your body. Notice the change? Write about it:

_____

_____

_____

_____

_____

Now cross it out with a giant X. What would you rather have happen next time? Write about it:

_____
_____
_____
_____

Trusting In The Order of Things 123...

What about trusting others, trusting in right timing, and that everything will work out even better than fine? This also comes back to trusting yourself. Because it means trusting that you're definitely making decisions that serve your greater good about what to do, when to do it, and who to put your faith in — in other words, having a keen sense of intuition. If you have ever been betrayed, this can be a tough one. And ooh, I would know. But what I learned, what ultimately made me realize that I was not helpless in these situations, was to see that betrayal is also self-betrayal. Why? Because it often means we didn't want to see or admit to ourselves the full truth of a situation. Which is hard to admit...BUT if this has happened to you, I'm willing to bet that you, like me, really know what to watch for next time, right? You also know you need to be more honest with yourself.

As a perfectionist, I have so many times struggled with being unable to change the past, unwilling to let go of mulling over all the times I've let myself down, why, how, etc. I really can't stand to steer myself wrong. But having been able to witness, through reading countless clients, how many of us really do get second and third chances over time, I have been willing to accept that I will eventually have the opportunity to reenact any situation in my life I choose, and that has helped me trust more and be more in the flow of the present moment and all the times it seemed like intuition has steered me in some weird way. Because if you believe in the perfection of all that is, if you believe that God or the Life-Force or the Universe or even nature really can't **do wrong**, well then, neither can you because we are made of the stuff of it.

It's important to trust in the greater **order of** things to sharpen your senses. Maybe your intuition leads you to a cool café **because** you have a vision of getting your work done there, but instead, you end up **sitting** next to a guy who chats with you the whole time you're supposed to be **working**. This actually happened as I was typing this, by the way. And let's say he **ends up** inspiring your project to go a whole different way. Happened too. Sometimes our spirit gives us the type of carrot (work, café) we're most likely to follow **to lead** us to things we may not have otherwise known we needed (new direction).

<u>Exercise</u>: *Trust In The Order Of Things*

Think of a day when you thought everything was going totally wrong, but it ended with a magical and most perfect surprise. Maybe you were late for a Yoga class you really wanted to try, got locked out, **and** ended up meeting a new best friend. Write about it here:

Re-Building Trust

Many of us have, over time, been invalidated in our intuition simply because this stuff was just not talked about. We weren't encouraged to follow it or believe in it. We may not even understand the full extent of what it is, what it means to have strong intuition, what it can do. Most of us weren't taught what it feels like to sense answers, to honor our ability to do so, to perceive the energy underlying things, so it's natural that you might have learned to mistrust it somewhat.

For a person like me who grew up sensitive, who always perceived energy before a word or action, life was super confusing. Because when a person's energy didn't match up with their words, on a really subtle level I started to mistrust people without knowing why. I mistrusted myself and the way I saw the world. I mistrusted the elders who were supposed to teach and protect me but were seemingly holding back some very important information, which drew more people to me that I couldn't trust, which made me mistrust myself even more, and the way I perceived the world. It wasn't until I spoke it out loud and honored my actual experience that things began to shift. I was honest about the fact that I was totally confused, and that opened the door to a whole new world for me.

And what about rebuilding trust in others? Well, in getting honest with myself that I hadn't been able to be honest with myself — because I didn't even understand what was going on until I fully surrendered to the fact I'd seen that future car accident behind my friend's head, which made me sick and really just seemed totally bizarre — I could accept it. And in doing so, I understood why, through deep experience, others seemingly did the same. I understood that we humans sometimes lie to ourselves when we don't have full understanding. And that doesn't excuse it, but acknowledging this allowed me to accept it. And that made it okay. It helped me to also forgive others when they'd seemingly been dishonest. And best of all, it meant I got to let go of the need to learn about dishonesty and mistrust. This meant it was no longer a big screaming sign in my energy field, and I no longer attract these lessons. To put it more bluntly: I saw that I — and I'm unfortunately not alone in this — sometimes had a tendency to lie to myself, to invalidate myself and my own intuition.

I've since turned this around and learned to trust in myself by validating the little wins. I have validated my intuition by getting to understand how I perceive energy. Through baby steps, I firmed up my self-confidence and rebuilt my self-trust. It's like a closed loop, really; work your sense of self-trust by working your intuition, work your intuition by working your sense of self-trust.

So, what's the easiest way to do this? Start by acknowledging, and thereby validating, an area in your life where your intuition is already strong. For instance, maybe you can't trust yourself to choose the right boss or the right partner, but can you trust yourself to order the perfect thing off a menu at a restaurant? Can you trust yourself to figure out how to get someplace without using GPS? Now, journal about it. Move your pen, move your hand, move some energy.

Exercise: Re-Building Self-Trust

Identify an area in your life where you've always been able to trust yourself, even if it's simply to know where you will always find the best chocolate cake or notice the prettiest flowers:

_____
_____
_____
_____
_____

Now, name one time in your life where everyone thought you'd be wrong, but you trusted your instincts completely, went against the grain, and were totally freaking dead on the money — it can even be a time when everyone ordered french fries and you ordered the sweet potato version, deciding they would be better, and they were. We're not going for magic here, just to get something down.

_____
_____
_____
_____
_____

Now if you really need to **rebuild** trust, write a journal entry every day for the next 30 days about one time you trusted yourself that day, and what happened as a result. At the end of your journal entry, close your eyes for a moment, think about the incident where you **trusted** yourself and feel what it feels like in your heart, in your body. Hold this feeling **for** 1-3 minutes to crystallize the experience.

The Dreaded Maybe's

What are some of the other blocks to self-trust? Indecision, or what I like to refer to as "the dreaded maybe" is another big one for us super intuitive fifth-dimensional beings who don't **want** to accept that we can't be in ten places at once...or maybe that's just me. (But I don't think so.) In a minute, we'll discuss what happens when "maybe" strikes. But first, we'll do an exercise so you can feel your clear "yes" and "no." Consider this your A/B test of intuition, which is good practice for validating and sharpening your senses when you're out in the world.

no. NO *yes* Yes! YES Yes. yes. YES. No! Yes. no. No.

no. NO *yes* Yes! YES No. no. Yes! No. No. Yes!

78

Intuition 101: Yes/No Answers

I recommend using this exercise to check in with yourself about small things — like turn right or left to find parking, fries vs. salad — then work up to bigger life decisions. This way, you're building self-trust through little intuitive wins. And because you're training yourself to feel it in your body, this will become easy over time, to the point you won't have to spend time mulling over the little things. Last, if you don't get anything at first, no biggie. Sometimes, we're just less inspired by certain subjects, so keep trying until you find something that speaks to you!

<u>**STEP 1**</u>: **Feel Your "Yes"**

Hold one hand in front of the other, palms facing in, about six inches from each other. Close your eyes and think of a person you love. Now imagine your outer hand was their hand, thinking about drawing it closer. Meditate on that person for a second, then shift the focus to your own body. Notice:

- How do you feel? Expanded? Light? Open? Another sensation?
- Where in your body do you feel the sensation most?
- How's your breathing?
- Do you get goose bumps, chills, or a tummy rumble?
- Do you hear a sound or an uplifting melody?
- Do you ee a visual symbol that depicts a clear "yes" answer?
- Do you taste or smell something you associate with positivity?

Hold that focus for a minute, feeling the sensation of "Yes" in your body.

<u>**STEP 2**</u>: **Feel Your "No"**

Now, keeping your hands where they are, shift focus to someone who you'd rather stay away — maybe it's a stranger on the street, an ex, an old boss that still rubs you the wrong way. Notice:

- How do you feel? Contracted? Tight? Closed off? Another sensation?
- Where in your body do you feel the sensation most?
- How's your breathing?
- Do you get goose bumps, chills, numbness or tummy trouble?
- Do you hear a sound or an ugly song?
- Do you see a visual symbol that depicts a clear "no" answer?
- So you taste or smell something you associate with negativity?

Hold that focus for a minute, feeling the sensation of "No" in your body.

STEP 3: Feel Your "Yes" Again!

Switch back to "Yes" so you can end on a good note. Now shake out your body, flutter your lips, and let it go. Journal about your experience, noting all the differences. Use often and repeat!

TIP: Did you have trouble finding your "Yes" and "No" using relationship examples? Or do you want to take this a step further? Try the exercise again, this time imagining you're doing your favorite hobby vs. something you can't stand doing. Or even test out a favorite food vs. one that makes you gag.

write!

_____

_____

_____

_____

_____

Defining Maybe

So, hopefully, from the previous exercise you've got a clear answer about how "Yes" and "No" feels in your body, how it looks, tastes and even smells. But what about all those times when you needed to make a super important decision, and all you could get out of your previously highly functioning intuition was "*Mmm*maybe?"

My favorite explanation comes from one of my teachers, who once used the example of having a jury inside. For the sake of keeping it simple, let's start with three important parts of yourself that help make intuitive decisions: mind, body and spirit. These are also known as third eye, gut, and heart-based intuition, respectively. What happens when they all want different things? Like, what if your third eye is interested in solo evening yoga, while your heart wants to focus on social time instead, and your gut just wants to cook a huge meal and get to bed early? In that case, who wins? Well, no one yet.

So you go consult some other important parts of yourself like your stomach, who wants avocado toast while you notice your texting fingers are already reaching out to some friends. Then you check with your heart again, who says a snack would be fine so long as you can go to a busy restaurant with whoever you just texted. And though your third eye's still urging you to get some space to reflect, it's feeling kind of noisy in your head. So your legs weigh in and tell you they were really loving the idea of some stretching. So sure you might have some direction now, but it definitely explains why you don't feel 100% about your choice. And if one team is wavering, or wants another outcome entirely? Now throw in all of the body's other intuitive centers and parts who want to weigh in with their needs and endless options and ideas. What if the decision is much more life-altering than cooking vs. yoga vs. friends? Well, you may be at a stalemate, my friend, waiting weeks for your final decision.

But hey, it's okay, because life is full and there's always another opportunity to make a different choice. So, maybe you are needing some social time, to stay out all night and party, even, but equally needing a good night's sleep. You might feel "*mmm*maybe" while your body's saying, hey, either one's good. Let's go for trial and error here, we can sleep another night, there will always be another party. Or another vacation or another apartment or another job and so on. "*Mmm*maybe" might just be trying to give you a balance of experiences, and if you think of it that way...well, it might not be so bad after all.

If you're really serious about curing your case of the "*mmm*maybe's," you can try the exercise on the next page. It comes from a super easy Qigong practice where you connect your three intuitive centers - third eye, heart, and gut - using a central line, kind of like an intuitive highway. You do it simply by closing your eyes and looking inward, imagining the line there. BUT in order to have it running smoothly, it's important to remember this: The part of "*mmm*maybe" that hurts you most is the self-judgment. If we don't accept ourselves as we are, we contract or cut off our own energy flow, which creates something like a bottleneck in our intuitive pathways. And it's *that* energy that interferes with intuition and leads us down uncomfy paths. So the moral of this story? "Maybe" is as "maybe" does. If you're getting "maybe," let go of judgment about yourself or fear of doing it wrong, and trust that your internal guidance system knows that either direction is perfectly worthwhile. Because you always get a second chance — not always with the same person in the same place at the same time, but if you haven't already noticed, the same stories in life play out over and over again until we're satisfied.

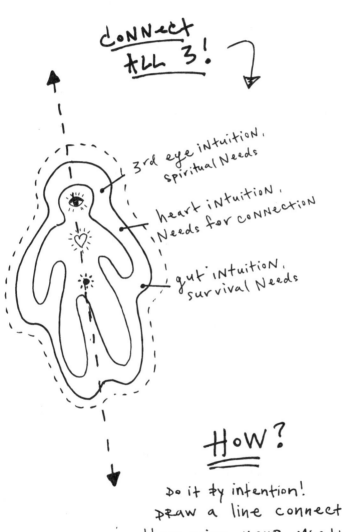

What If You're Just Making It Up?

So what if you can't tell if you're listening to the voice of your intuition or one you might be making up? There was a time I kept messing up the directions to a Yoga class I really wanted to try, only to find out later that the teacher was inappropriate with female students, and by not going, I'd totally dodged a bullet. And this has happened to me many times — where I randomly got lost or distracted and simply didn't show up to a situation that wouldn't have been good for me. And I didn't even need to feel scared or worried or even get a detailed message about what to do to stay out of trouble...all I had to do was be my regular day-dreamy self. All you have to do is just decide to trust and let go of needing to know why.

And how do you tell the difference between intuition, thoughts, ideas, and emotion? We'll get to that when we talk about what to do to clear up that potentially foggy lens of perception. This piece comes as you get more familiar with what it feels like to have a super clear intuitive hit based on your own truth vs. a learned thought or emotion. But do you know what has to come before this? Deciding that you're definitely not making it up and giving yourself permission to play with this stuff in the first place.

Giving Yourself Permission

It was 11:11 on a Sunday at brunch, and Tania suggested we make a wish. I asked the Universe for help with this writing, which I'd totally been avoiding that day. Not a minute later, my friend Edan started to tell a story about a time in his life when he saw 11:11 everywhere. What seemed crazier, especially for a fairly conservative finance man like him, was that for months since he'd returned from a Yoga retreat in India, whenever he'd walk underneath a streetlight, it would go out. At first he passed it off as coincidence, but when it became the family joke, he needed to know why. After all, his was a world of logic, math and answers.

Not too long after he'd asked, of course, the answer came to him in the form of an email. Someone had sent him a video of a famous illusionist who was known as a magician and worker of energy — someone who was definitely in the know about situations like these. And so Edan wrote him to see if he could offer some insight. The next morning, Edan woke up to find a message on his screen, a reply from the man himself, who suggested he look up something called Streetlight Interference. Of course, Edan thought it was crazy, but the name certainly fit what kept happening. And so he Googled it, and of course it is a thing, possibly the result of Edan's specific frequency. But what message did it serve to give him? That, he didn't know.

A few days later, Edan received a follow-up message from the magician: Soon you'll be seeing double numbers everywhere. Sure enough, he did. And with that, Edan started to feel he was losing his grip on the reality he knew so well, one that he was not ready to change. He wanted a life he could explain to his friends and relatives, not to be the butt of a joke he couldn't explain. He wanted logic, facts, straightforward messages, not an existence that involved following signs. And when he said so out loud, it stopped. Soon, streetlights stayed on when he walked under them, he no longer saw patterns and 11:11s. Which, for him, meant his world was back to normal. Well, his version of it anyway. In a sense, he'd chosen to revoke his permission to follow energies and intuition — because the choice of what to believe in, where we want to put our faith, focus, and trust, is ours.

So what are some other forms of permission? Just as Edan's permission slip had come via a spiritual retreat, my friend Tania's came in medicinal form when she joined a plant medicine ceremony for purging and clarity. She did it just once, kept what she needed in the form of "knowings" — smells, mostly, and body sensations — an ability she retained for years after. When asked about it, she'll say she felt her keen sense for perception had always been there, but the medicine was what had granted her permission to use it.

My own permission slip that led to the reclamation of my intuitive abilities came from neither guru nor substance, but from a conversation I had with a tree. Yup. Totally sober and feeling stuck in my life, I did that brutal surrender thing by going outside to pray. Through tears, I looked to my favorite old oak and asked her if she had answers for me. Surprisingly, she spoke back. And it jarred me out of the fog I'd been feeling for so long. That type of permission slip was exactly what I needed to remember that my world has all the answers I need to know.

Do you remember one of yours? If not, that's okay, because of course I have an exercise to open this up down below. Because your permission can come from anywhere, so long as you truly want it. All you need is the willingness to open more to what you've already got. And like Edan, know that you can close it off again if you like. We are the masters of our own experience, we are the ones driving our bodies. Are you ready?

<u>Exercise</u>: *Your Permission Slip*

So now it's your turn. Why wait for a crisis, a substance, or a guru to tell you what you already know? Chances are all you need is proof, and if you ask nicely, you will get it. So get out a pen and some paper and write a little note to the Uni, specifying that you hereby give yourself permission. It can go a little something like:

Dear Universe / Good Creative Force / Your Name Here,

I hereby recognize myself as an Intuitive, Sensitive, Psychic, and Super Perceptive human. I know I have the ability to receive helpful messages from the unknown, especially judging from this _____(insert crazy coincidence-laden story here)____ that I never could quite explain. Whether or not that was an intuitive communication, I'm going to label it as such because, hey, this is a private letter and I have nothing to lose, but I badly want to deepen my sense of trust. I experienced _____ (cool coincidence) with my own _____(insert sense here, such as eyes, nose, ears)____ and I promise to pay extra close attention to the other subtle messages I can get in much the same way. So please send a sign today, as I will be looking for it. Maybe it can even be in the form of a _____(insert fun idea here, like finding a magic feather)____ or otherwise surprise me :). Thank you so much for your efforts thus far and I look forward to hearing from you soon.

With unconditional love and gratitude,
(Your Name Here Too) _____

...Then, journal for the next 24 hours and see what comes up!

All Are Called, Few Choose To Listen.
BUT...How Do We Listen?

So here's something you may have noticed in the story with Edan, but if not, I should probably point it out. Did any of you catch how my wish came true not 30 seconds after I made it? I'm not bringing this up to brag, but to offer you a very useful tool and another little nudge if you still haven't composed your letter. Because ever since I started paying attention to the signs, really using my intuition to the best of my ability, magic has happened in the form of synchronicities such as that one, or what I like to refer to as little miracles, every day so long as I have asked out loud. And that has really built up my trust. Did I expect to be working on my project that day at brunch? No. But because I chose to pay attention and be open to whatever came, some force out there decided to smile on me as I ate my eggs. I was gifted with a beautiful story that not only gave me insight I could eventually share, but gave me the encouragement I needed to keep going on this path. When you open up to sensing, you open yourself to guidance and greater faith. And I write that just as much as a reminder to you as to myself. And sure, sometimes the help doesn't come exactly in the way you'd expect, but it always comes.

the Clairs

3.

On Becoming Egg-Voyant

Amber was dating a guy she was crazy about — a guy who, well, pretty much made her crazy. When he'd show up two hours late for their dates or sometimes not at all, she'd break up with him, read every self-help book known to woman, meet someone else, feel totally happy...until he showed up at her door again with a cool song he wrote or a poem about why he couldn't live without her. It was that sort of thing.

One night, when they were back together again, she invited him for dinner with a bunch of friends. After 15 minutes of waiting for him to show, she put her phone out on the table. After 30 minutes, she flipped it over so no one could see he hadn't replied. And when an hour passed, she excused herself from the table to go to the bathroom and cry. The worst part, of course, was she still badly wanted to see him. She made it through dinner and excused herself from drinks afterwards. Once she was in bed, makeup-less, and feeling sorry for herself, she heard a knock at the door. And it doesn't take a psychic to know it was him. She managed to wait at least 30 seconds, but she jumped out of bed and ran for the door. She turned the handle a bit and he pushed it wide open, almost knocking her to the ground, then started on a long-winded story about what'd happened to him that night. She didn't even hear it — her ears ringing like alarm bells. And anyway, it was probably something like the usual, "Sorry, babe, but my phone died and..." Still, she went to kiss him. And that's when he turned his face and said, "You know, babe, I'm really hungry. Would you mind making me something to eat?" She agreed.

"I think I just wanted to be alone with the knives," she told me later. Amber looked in the fridge, but all she had was eggs. And so she heated up some butter, stared into the pan, and prayed for help to see what it was she couldn't. "Please, universe," she whispered, "tell me what it is about—" And before she could finish, she'd cracked open a stinking, rotting egg.

So, Is Being Egg-Voyant A Thing Then?

You may be asking whether this falls under the category of intuition. Well, if intuition is about reading the signs, the energy, getting hunches and clues that logic can later test out, then I'd have to ask, How is it not? The bigger question is: What exactly do we file this type of scenario under? And how do we get more access to helpful clues like that? As you develop and expand your capacity for intuition, it's helpful to pay attention to how you pick up on subtle information. And while I'm sure there's a tradition somewhere in the world for reading late-night eggs, just as reading tea leaves and coffee grounds are a thing, we'll file Amber's story under clairvoyance.

So, in this chapter, we're going to explore the different ways we each sense energy so you can understand how it shows up for you. Are you clairvoyant, for example? Claircognizantly knowing what you empathically feel and clairsentiently experience while you remote view from across the world? Channel guidance through dreams and mediumship? Or do you have zero idea what I just said, but think these sound exactly like the type of superpowers you came here for? Here I'll get into terminology. Because giving voice to how you sense energy opens up the pathways for more. And by the end, you'll have a clear idea of how you experience energy, by using one of the most important exercises, one I'll refer to again and again in this book and use almost daily for feeling and balancing energy, for "plugging in."

The Clairs

When I think of the word "clairvoyant," it still brings up memories of neon window signs on downtown street corners in the city where I grew up. But, really it's French: *clair* means "clear," and *voyant* refers to "seeing." And while the next chapters are all about how to see more clearly — because, let's face it, sometimes we can interpret the world through a pretty foggy lens — first, we have to talk about what it means to "see" in this context. Literally, Amber saw that disgusting egg and got her message pretty freaking clearly. Does it matter whether she saw the thing in the middle of her mind's eye or in a frying pan? I'll let you decide. The point is, she got the message.

So, let's take a look at how we intuit information, since we all pick up on subtle energy cues differently. Just like I may be more visual while you thrive on words, we're all gifted with sense perception in different ways. And while clairvoyance is one of the more familiar words associated with intuition, it's not the only way we can perceive. As you go through these, I recommend taking note of experiences you've had — through journaling or speaking them out loud. Acknowledgment is key to opening up to more ways of receiving information in greater detail.

Clairvoyance

Do you tend to describe things using imagery? Does visual harmony make your heart sing? If you tend to favor your visual sense, then you are most likely clairvoyant. Energetic information can show up clairvoyantly through drawing or dreaming, seeing symbols, colors, textures, or imagery in your inner mind's eye or external world, with eyes open or closed. You may actually see colors, shapes, or textures surrounding a person, for example, or notice symbols in your environment like a meaningful object, picture, sentence, sign or significant visual change in your space that happens after you've posed a question. Or you may see light, patterns, and images while sitting in meditation with eyes closed, focused on your inner world.

My friend Sarah loves to decorate. When she came over upset and unable to make a decision about a new job, she asked me for advice. But when she finished pouring her heart out, I had nothing. We sat on the couch for a while, silent, staring at each other. Soon, her eyes went to my coffee table. "What's this book?" She said, reaching for a blue hardcover with a picture of a butterfly on the spine. She pulled it out and read the back. Of course, it was a quote by Neil Gaiman with the perfectly worded answer to the question she'd just asked. And she'd seen the answer sitting right on my coffee table, first intuitively and then in printed words.

Others who are clairvoyant might doodle to help them clear their mind and notice that they're drawing the answer! In fact, one of the classic techniques taught for Remote Viewing, a methodical practice which focuses on getting information about something happening far away, involves scribbling a line. So, how does your clairvoyance show up?

Oh and fun side note...after Sarah found her answer, she took the book home. A few weeks later, I was having some writer's block and decided to walk down the hill to my favorite bookstore. I grabbed the same book and took it home. En route, I flipped the book over and read the Neil Gaiman quote on the back. Not only was it a different quote, but it had to do with exactly what I'd been struggling with that day! Different edition? Maybe. I like to think it was a little bit of magic.

Clairaudience

Are you an audiophile? Do you understand the world through sound? Many people hear words, sentences or vibrations containing guidance and information. If you love music, you might notice a meaningful song or lyric pops into your head or plays nearby as you think about a question that needs answering. Many of us sense the rhythm of words; often, we know someone's holding back truth by the tone of their voice.

Layla is a DJ, totally obsessed with music and she's also a super intuitive sister. When I asked how she gets her knowings, she said she can always tell within the first sentence of an email if her rhythm will vibe well with the person who's writing to her. So much so, that recently she decided to pick and choose her clients based on the rhythms of their emails alone. And since then, she's had no issues with anyone she's chosen to work with. This is a perfect example of clairaudience showing up in ways we might not expect.

Here's another example: I was dating a guy, feeling unsure about him. I was about to message him back when another text came through from a friend. It was a song called "Dance Alone"! Still curious and always excited to connect with people, I went to click the guy's name to make plans, when the song started playing on its own. I laughed, danced to it a bit (hey, I had to follow instructions) then deleted the text to him and thanked my friend and our guides for the warning.

And remember how Amber had heard alarm bells ringing instead of her man's story? That's an example of clairaudience too. Sometimes I hear a bell when something "rings true," whether they come from a phantom source or an actual bell in the room. Automatic speaking — letting words spill out without giving them thought — also falls into this category. These are just some of the forms clairaudience can take. How does it show up for you?

Clairsentience

Do you thrive on physical activity? Feel the heavy sensations of intuition in your gut? Most of us perceive energetic information through feeling. For example, lots of us have experienced a knowing feeling in our tummy, shivers, or goose bumps even when it's not cold, or a tightening in the chest when we're about to get into a situation we don't like. If you pay attention, it's easy to sense energy through the palms of your hands, which is sometimes referred to as psychometry, but perhaps more popularly known through hands-on energy practices like Reiki. The hands are said to be an extension of our heart. Do you feel sluggish around someone who pushes your buttons, and energetic around someone you like? Have you ever followed your feet and ended up in exactly the right place at the right time?

Ed is one of the most heart-centered people I know. When he had throat surgery and wasn't allowed to talk for a week, he had to resort to using the rest of his body for social time and communication. He'd been thinking about buying a home for a while, but he felt like it was almost foolish to look, living in New York with its tough housing market. But after Sunday brunch with his friends ended, he wanted to keep hanging out and needed an activity. So off they went, looking at houses.

Totally silently, he followed his feet down the hill and wandered around the block past what looked like an open house. He turned to his friends, shrugged, and walked in. Somehow, they were the only people there that morning, and it turned out to be exactly the type of house he'd always dreamed of living in — it was the perfect place for entertaining. He made an offer that afternoon (in writing of course) and moved in a few weeks later. That, my friends, is a brilliant example of getting guidance through clairsentience.

And have you ever had phantom pains in the body? Even discovered later that someone close to you was experiencing a similar issue at the time? Or aches that show up only around certain situations or people? I thought I had an issue with my neck until I realized it only hurt while working a job I didn't like. Literally, that situation was a pain in the neck. How does clairsentience show up for you?

Claircognizance

Are you someone who daydreams and likes to think through even the littlest details? Do you get a ton of ideas or simply know things without knowing how you know? Do you tend to call or text a friend out of the blue and then they tell you they'd just been thinking of you? Do people tell you that you said what they needed to hear at exactly the time they needed to hear it? Are you able to answer your own questions through automatic writing — as in picking up a pen, just writing what comes? These are all examples of claircognizance. And while many of us receive information this way, it can be tricky to validate. When we get to reading others and receiving feedback on our knowings, you might learn how claircognizant you really are! How has claircognizance showed up for you?

Clairgustance

Yup, this is a thing. Our sense of taste gives helpful clues about energy too. Does someone leave a phantom bitter taste in your mouth while you think of another person as sweet, and literally taste candy? If your sense of taste is well developed, you can use these types of cues to get information.

For me, clairgustant signals come up specifically to give clues about relationships. For example, my friend Kelly and I once had an epic night that ended with the best slice of pizza both of us had ever had. Since then, I taste pizza when I'm about to get a text from her. Sometimes, when I'm reading for others and I taste flavors that remind me of childhood, it tells me to look more deeply into their past. This one's not super common, mainly because most of us don't experience the world by walking around licking everything. So don't worry if this isn't a thing you've experienced, but why not take a second to think how it might be?

Clairsalience

Clairsalience is similar to getting information through taste, but with smell. Does something smell fishy? Then it probably is. Perhaps your clairsalience is more subtle; even sensing a change in your own breathing can give a hint. Do you avoid inhaling deeply around certain people, places, or things? Does a person's space, and therefore its energy, smell stale and you can't wait to leave, open a window, and let freshness in? Or do you feel you can breathe a little better in certain places? Does the air smell like perfume around certain people?

My mom's always been hung up on smells, be it the scent of certain foods or energy lingering in her space once a person's left it. Growing up, I'd see her walking around the house wiggling her nose with cleaning supplies in her hand. Extreme, yes. But if we vibe well with a scent, it's usually a good indicator that we like the energy. And then there are phantom smells that can give us information too. I often smell someone's scent when they've later said they were thinking of me, even if they weren't anywhere close by, just before they've texted or called. And when someone's not telling the truth, well, sometimes I smell the faint but off-putting scent of BS. Has clairsalience ever shown up for you?

Clairempathy

Are you someone who feels into the depth and detail of every emotion, even ones that don't feel like they belong to you? If so, this may be one of your primary methods of intuition. It can feel scary at times to experience what seems like the emotion of another, but as we'll get into later, there are ways to curb it — and anyway, it's impossible to feel energy you don't share with another in at least some capacity. Emotional energy can be useful to sense. There's a wealth of information about your surroundings, relationships, and even your own personal path buried within it.

So how does this show up in life? Well, chances are that if you're clairempathic, you already know you are. How? In extreme cases, you could be someone who feels tossed around by emotion like you're in a washing machine. Or maybe you feel down after watching the news, anxious around stressed out people, high on life coming home from a fun night out with friends. I believe we all sense each other's feelings to some degree. And I'm not sure there's much difference between being an Empath and being clairempathic other than the being-clear-on-what-you-sense part. Some of us are just more aware of it than others. I once heard Marianne Williamson say something along the lines of, "If you don't feel sad about the state of the world after watching a depressing news cycle, then there's probably something wrong."

The reason I think we can all easily relate to clairempathy is while the English language doesn't have a ton of words for describing patterns of subtle energy, we do have words for emotions — and since they have no material form, it's pretty safe to say they're energy. So, my guess is that because we're more familiar with the energetic pattern of, say, "sadness" than the energetic pattern of "He's feeling down and confused about quitting his job because it's no longer inspiring him," it's easy for most of us to tap into clairempathy. How have you experienced it?

Putting It All Together

Often, we intuit subtle, energetic information using a combination of all of these. And maybe you've even noticed that different sorts of information — for example, info about relationships vs. career stuff — comes in different ways. Paying attention with conscious awareness not only helps us know where to look when we're in need of guidance, but it also helps us to open up and develop other clair-senses we have but aren't aware of yet. Keeping a journal about your daily or weekly intuitive sensing is helpful for further discovery.

CLAIR COUSINS: Mediumship, Remote Viewing, Channeling, Dreaming & Reading Anything... From Our Pets To Akashic Records!

Now I bet you're wondering about other words associated with intuition, like psychic, medium, medical medium, channeling, remote viewing, spirit guides, angels, animal communication, Akashic Record reading, past lives, soul retrieving, Reiki, energy healing...and a whole bunch of others I'm probably not aware of yet that exist to describe what seems indescribable. For the sake of keeping it brief, I'll say these titles usually refer to a specialty — kind of like how a doctor may choose to become a pediatrician because they happen to be great with kids. I've always been good at forecasting trends and so I often see trajectories of energy too, which makes me a pretty good psychic. I like to help people and I'm fascinated by life purpose, which means I get energy healing and Akashic Records stuff coming through, too. But while I love animals, I don't have a strong affinity with them, so I don't tend to pick up on messages from beloved pets unless someone asks me to.

As humans, we tend to focus on what we like. If you're open enough, any or all of this type of information is available to you. And since I brought it up, I'll say that the difference between reading pets and reading the Akashic Records is simply the source of your information. In one case, you're asking the spirit of what you once knew as your cute kitty Bobo to come through, for instance, and in the other, you're requesting a connection to something that, to me, resembles something like a giant library with information about soul paths and learning over lifetimes. It's like deciding which friend to call for the type of advice you're looking for. And with psychic predictions? Well, anyone who can sense energy can know what's coming. Because if thought creates form, then energy shapes future reality.

Mediumship

The word "mediumship" has been used to refer both to the method in which we download information and to the act of communicating with an ancestor or friend in spirit. Classic mediumship has involved candlelit seances in dark rooms, channeling spirits through the Medium's body, vocal changes, drama, but it's not necessary. Personally, I don't enjoy foreign-feeling energy patterns in my body, nor the big shifts associated with acting as someone other than myself, but I can still read the energy of a loved one who's passed. In other words, I practice mediumship — because I do connect to spirits — but I do it without making my body into the medium, or vessel, in which the energy comes through. I simply take a look at the energy like I'm watching a movie, if that makes sense.

Let's say you see a guy smoking a pipe and wonder if it belonged to his grandfather — this is an example of mediumship because you are connecting in some way to the energy of a person who's passed over. And while a well-practiced Medium may actually "know" about the type of connection this man had with his grandfather, perceive the grandfather as "close by" to be able to deliver a specific message, relay fine details, or even channel the energy through his or her body and take on the voice or mannerisms of the grandfather...well, the point is, we all have access to this sort of information in different capacities. I find that many friends and clients communicate with their own ancestors in dreams or through doing activities they shared and loved. I communicate with my grandmother when I'm cooking, for example, because it's something we always did together.

Channeling & Telepathy

Channeling is another method, very similar to what I just described. Rather than holding the energy in our bodies like a classic Medium would, "channeling" means passing it through. The word itself refers to something that gets something else from one place to another. You can use a straw to channel juice from a cup to your mouth, channel an idea through your body, chennel ink out of a pen onto paper, for example. You can use it to describe what happens when you tap into wisdom from your higher, more intelligent, all-knowing, wise spirit self as it applies to your Earthly day-to-day self. It all works.

The act of channeling does not necessarily mean communicating with characters from other realms, although it can. To me, channeling simply feels like energy moving through my body — like the feeling I get when I'm really in the flow making art, when I get an idea and execute it smoothly, and of course when I knowingly or unknowingly say the very thing a person needed to hear. So how do you become a channel? Easy! First, you acknowledge that you already are — just think of any time you brought an idea (a bit of energy) through to physical form. If you have ever, say, decided to build a birdhouse and then built one, you technically channeled that idea from the ether through your brain and out of your hands.

Of course, becoming a clear channel is something else. Because when you move something from point A to point B, you want the path to be as clean as possible so the thing doesn't get dirtied up along the way. In the next chapter, we'll discuss good ways to clear. Telepathy — or the ability to pick up someone else's thoughts — could also fall into this category. Because if our ideas come from the ether, can anyone really claim ownership over them? Just something to think about.

Remote Viewing, Astral Travel, Dreaming & Reading Anything, Really

Remote viewing is yet another method of reading energy, and it's often done under a strict set of rules that involves recording information within a given time period. The method is exact, goes beyond the scope of this book, and is actually one of the rare cases when someone could technically do intuition wrong — if you're interested, more resources are listed on my site. For now, I will say that this is a method usually used to gather information about a faraway location. I don't read this way because I'm just not that into rules, but remote viewing is an excellent way to find things like lost car keys, so if you have a talent and an interest, go for it.

Astral travel is something like taking your energy body for a ride. It also goes beyond the scope of this book, because I'm not a fan of leaving my physical body to go traveling and this book focuses on the ways to read energy while staying in our bodies; anything else just doesn't feel good to me. But I will say that many of us sensitive people sometimes astral travel by accident, often while we're asleep. And you might know if you're doing this because usually those types of "dreams" have a different quality to them. Perhaps this happens a bit differently for each of us.

I know that I'm traveling during dreaming when I'm looking at a room from a bird's eye view, hearing muffled voices, and seeing light much brighter than I see it during the day. I've accidentally astral traveled to the birthing rooms of some of my friends. How do I know? Because I woke up after "dreaming" they'd given birth only to discover they actually had. Why does this happen? My guess is probably because I'm a friend who likes to offer support and also be in exciting places. If you suffer from sleepless nights due to accidental astral travel, try the exercise for plugging in and grounding your energy at the end of this chapter before going to bed at night. And if you want to know how to travel, see my website for resources.

Many of us receive guidance through dreams. There are periods of our dream-state where we go in alpha-theta brainwaves, which is the same state we strive for when meditating to consciously do this work. And because we're so relaxed and non-judgmental of ourselves while we're sleeping, it's a good opportunity to feel comfortable with being receptive. One of my clairvoyance teachers says the best way to experience guidance through dreaming is simply by acknowledging it. For best results, write out an intention before bed, ask a question, and when you wake up, make sure to journal the answer, even if nothing came. With time and patience, the details come. And opening to receiving guidance through dream-space is a great way to open up to getting signs in waking life too.

So you see, there are so many ways to read energy. We all do what resonates with us. And as I've said, this book focuses mostly on reading while experiencing our own energy in our own bodies. It works for reading any bit of energy — from a loved one who's passed over, an object, a puppy, even your next date...even though that's not always recommended. Soon we're going to try it. But first, here's a little story about one of my early practice readings.

Phone Troubles

The first time I got confirmation that I communicated with a deceased person I'd never met before, it took me by surprise. I was practicing reading with a volunteer — let's call her Tammy — and she wanted to know about her relationship with a guy she was seeing who was very much alive. We'll call him Larry. As you'll learn to do a little later, I set up my psychic toolkit and asked her to say the name of her current beau. "MNeeehhrD." I heard. The phone seemed to cut out a bit, so I asked her to repeat herself. She apologized over a totally clear phone line in a sweet Minnesota tone, but when she tried to say the guy's name again, all I heard was "MNNehhhdDDrrd," and a whole bunch of fuzz.

Frustrated and wanting to do a good reading, I finally said whatever I thought I heard: "You say his name is Ned?" The static on my phone died down and suddenly I heard nothing. My face felt hot. I moved my phone around, thinking I needed to angle it for better reception. Finally, I heard a sound on the other end of the line as she started to chuckle. "Well...wow...this is odd," Tammy said. "But I guess I should tell you that my first husband's name was Ned. But he's passed away. And you know what? He wouldn't like Larry for me at all." She thanked me for the answer I didn't even really give, and for reminding her of her loving connection with Ned. I told her I thought I was just having phone issues, and we both laughed at the strangeness of it all.

So, you see, there's no rule about how our intuitive senses show up. And we don't always know what's going to come through — that's where getting confirmation is helpful. Now, you may already be thinking back to experiences you've had where you knew something about someone's health condition or had a hunch about where your mom left her phone. And if so, speak it out loud or write it down! It's helpful to start to notice where strong intuition kicks in, because it all boils down to what interests you, your intention, where your focus is, how important the information is that you're picking up. In my own experience of reading, I know that certain details — for instance, about a deceased husband or pet goldfish (yes, I once read a goldfish) — will come up if it's relevant to the reading.

And why does it help to understand your clair-potential? So you know how to receive the information that's available to you when you tune into yourself for guidance. And if you're sensitive and pick up a lot, it's helpful to be aware of when you're picking up information, so you can make a choice whether to respond to it or not. It's not about learning how to read energy so you can spy on people — we'll discuss ethics when we get into reading others — but about learning how we're *already* reading it, so we can better understand our relationships with others and ourselves, with the energy surrounding us. If there is something that makes you uncomfy, such as mediumship or "seeing" news you'd rather not see, you can choose not to engage with it and it simply won't show up.

SO...Let's Play With Energy!

Now, enough of me talking about this stuff — it's time to experience it for yourself. So, now is when we get into tools for working with energy! This first one is crucial for aligning your own intuition and clearing pathways so energy can move through you in a balanced way. I'm going to refer to this exercise again and again as the first step for almost every energy tool I'll share. In fact, if this is the only practice you do, it will help you feel more in sync with yourself, balanced and centered on a daily basis. It's easiest to start with your eyes closed so you can better focus on your inner world without distraction.

As with many things that run on electricity, we're going to set ourselves up like a three-pronged plug so we're evenly connected, plugged into a natural source of energy: the world around us. The feeling will be subtle. We'll run a positive charge (your connection to the Universe or Cosmic Energy), a negative charge (your connection to Earth Energy), and a neutral ground that I'll refer to as a Grounding Cord (connection to the Center of the Earth) — which is like a lightning rod that directs energy down into Big Mama Earth. Earth center is neutral because it's right in the middle, so it doesn't sway to either polarity.

As I mentioned, this practice is so helpful for balancing ourselves out. Many of us are either stuck up in our heads, floating off in the ether, in our spiritual realms, or thinking too much, while others are too often stuck in the material reality, focused only on survival and physical needs, when what we all want, for best results, is to have a balance of both. That way, you can intuitively find a job that also gives you a sense of purpose. A romantic partner that feeds your soul. Or if you tend to float off and daydream with hundreds of ideas that never seem to materialize, or if you love to work but never have new ideas... well, this works for that too. And of course, this is the first step to reading your own energy — so you have access to the <u>full</u> scope of it — and it's eventually how you'll read pretty much anything else too. The first step is to align your energy within yourself.

So if you do this, it won't really feel like lightning at all. In fact, it's pretty subtle. But you may feel more energized, you may feel energy moving, lighter or heavier than before, or sleepy if you were tired but trying not to notice it. It's also possible that the sensation's so subtle you'll feel nothing at all. If that's the case, just keep at it and you will. If you feel dizzy, it's probably a result of moving energy blocks, and if that happens, you'll want to shake out your body and drink lots of water. Shaking helps reset, water moves energy.

If it does feel uncomfortable for a bit, you can ease your head by reminding yourself that we are creatures of the earth below and sky above and nurturing the connection to our natural surroundings is, well, natural. So there's nothing to fear here. Except for maybe greater knowing and feeling more aligned with yourself and the greater whole, which (if you ask me) is only scary if you're not up for feeling pretty good most of the time. So here we go on this fun and personally empowering ride of working with energy!

eNeRgy aNatoMy 101

* We can 'plug iN' just like a 3-PRoNg Plug!

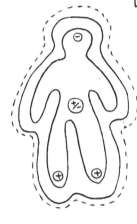 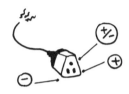

* the eaRth's CeNteR is betweeN 2 polarities! and so... it's Neutral!

* ouR CeNteR is Neutral too!

...So why Not Plug iN YouR eNeRgy?

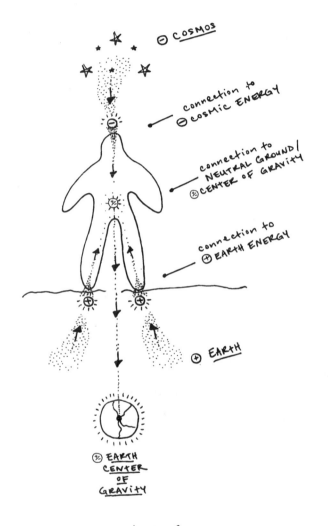

ENERGY TOOL #1:
Plugging In Your Energy

To Open: Pay Attention to Your Body...AKA Posture

Sit with both soles of your feet touching the floor, spine upright. It's helpful to sit on a stool or corner of a chair, so your core is engaged and allowing more energy to flow through your torso. You can also stand and do this. It's easier to start with your eyes closed, to focus on perceiving the energy running through the inside of your body, rather than on the external world. For best results, do this for at least 12 minutes, two times per day. Think of it as an energy clearing and resetting meditation. Once you feel your energy running, relax and let it flow.

STEP 1: Connect to Earth Center — Your Neutral Ground

A. Put both hands over your center of gravity, below your navel, between the front and back of your body; you can find the exact spot intuitively. Breathe your belly out into the palm of your hands, and slowly begin to push all four sides of your body out from the inside, so you're expanding and creating space with every inhale. Feel your Core Center, the warmth below your hands. If you're visual, you can imagine a glowing ball of light there, like your very own personal sun — a ball of light that has weight and density to it, like the center of the Earth.

B. Now imagine a cord connecting your Core Center of gravity to the Earth's. If you can't visualize or feel it, you can simply set the intention. This is your Grounding Cord. You can get creative with it: visualize or feel that Grounding Cord as a candy cane or a slide, or decorate it with sparkles — whatever will make your heart smile in this moment.

C. Sit with it for a minute or two, feeling the weight of your body tethered to the Earth. Don't try too hard. For best results, just allow, observe, have fun.

STEP 2: Connect to Earth Energy — Your Negative Charge

A. Shift your focus to the soles of your feet, imagining you have spinning doors on them that, when open, allow energy in and out. Imagine them opening up wide.

B. Imagine sprouting roots like a tree out the soles of your feet, down into the Earth, finding a pure place from which to gather energy that perfectly suits you today — it can be from anywhere on this Earth! If you're clairvoyant, you can "watch" the roots drop down through several layers of dirt, finding the good stuff. If you're more clairsentient, feel your feet heavy on the floor.

C. Pull up Earth Energy through your feet. You can give it a color and watch or just feel as it spirals up through the feet, past the ankles, calves, knees, thighs, hips, and pelvic floor until it's swishing around your Core Center in the lower torso.

D. Allow that energy to flow back down into the Earth via your Grounding Cord. It will take with it bits of old stagnant energy you were storing — your body's energy system is intelligent and knows what to do, what it needs to keep and what it needs to release. You may feel some sensation associated with this.

E. Sit with it and feel, allowing the energy to run through you. Set the intention to keep this going, even if you're not focusing on it.

STEP 3: Connect to Cosmic Energy — Your Positive Charge

A. Shift your focus to the crown of your head, imagining you have a spinning door that, when open, allows energy in and out. Imagine opening it up wide.

B. Imagine a pure place of energy out in the cosmos that's perfectly suited for you and your highest good today. I often connect to the North Star, Vega, or a galaxy I see in my mind's eye.

C. Now, invite it in. You can give it a color or texture, and watch or feel as it spirals down through the crown, face, back of the head, neck, throat, over the heart, upper back, chest front and back, arms, hands, rib cage, diaphragm, middle torso, solar plexus, sacrum, and lower back until it meets the Earth Energy swishing around your Core Center in the lower torso.

D. Allow that energy to flow straight down into the Earth via your Ground, along with any old stagnant energy you were storing. Sit with it and feel, allowing the energy to run through you. Do you notice a difference between Earth Energy and Cosmic Energy?

STEP 4: Clear Your Core Central Energy Channel

A. Imagine your Core Channel in the center of your body, like a pathway or tube that connects your crown, heart, and Core Center. It can reach all the way up to the cosmos, and all the way down to the Earth Center via your Grounding Cord.

B. Imagine collecting the perfect mixture of Earth Energy and Cosmic Energy from your lower torso, and spiral it up through your Core Channel, spouting it out the crown, and back down around the sides of where you imagine the boundaries of your aura to be. It's like having a protective cocoon of energy around you, cleaning off the insides.

C. Allow excess energy to drip back down into the Earth.

D. Sit with it, feel and notice your sensations.

To Close: Journal

Give voice to your experience: How does your body feel? What are your emotions saying? Did any images, visuals, or memories come up? Maybe you didn't notice that much, other than a new sensation in your toenail, and that's fine so long as you record the details. And how did you perceive the energy: Was it clairvoyantly? Clairsentiently? Clairaudiently? Maybe you didn't feel it at all, but it just felt good, in which case you sensed clairempathically. Journal at least 5 minutes, as if recording the details of a dream — sometimes it takes time for it all to come back to you. And if you didn't feel much, just do less next time — that's when we're most receptive!

write!

_____
_____
_____
_____
_____

Did Anyone See Christopher Columbus Sailing The Ocean Blue?

There's an old Captain Cook ship's log that says as Christopher Columbus' ships sailed for the shores of Australia, the aboriginals could not see the ships coming. It's not that no one was at the beach that day — it's just that they'd never seen a fleet like that and so the entire scene did not register. Or so the story goes, anyway. For many of us, our experience of subtle energy, and often the experience of a subtle energy shift, is somewhat similar. Without having had a tangible, provable experience of feeling energy, it sometimes doesn't register. Because we don't know what to look for, we may not know that it (whatever *it* may be) is happening! So practice, believe, and pay attention to the details and little wins.

CLaiR·iNG
YOUR
LeNS

4.

Reading Through A Smudgy Lens

It was Sunday morning and I was practicing reading with two other psychic sisters over the phone. Our client was asking for help in her relationship. We set the energetic space, spoke our intentions, and then tuned in remotely to read as a group. I began the reading by taking a look at my client's essence and "saw" her aura shining bright pink, feeling her nurturing warmth. We sat for a moment before she brought up her relationship. When she did, her energy contracted. It shrank and suddenly felt cold. I watched as her subtle body started to slump forward, like she'd been blindsided, punched in the gut. And whether she was bent that way physically, emotionally, or some other way wasn't clear, so I paused and asked for some guidance. What came through was a message to share tools that would build up her energy. And so I sat in my meditative space, watching as images popped up: her at the gym, out with friends, listening to her favorite songs. I was about to share when another reader, Shaya, burst out, "Oh my God girl, get out of that relationship — RUN!" Shocked, I sat in silence, centering myself.

I watched as the client's energy body went from slumped to barely there. The third reader chimed in and changed the subject. But our client's energy never bounced back. After she got off the call, we readers stayed on to debrief. And that's when Shaya told us she'd been in an abusive relationship — which was not surprising, given the way she spoke about what she saw. Our client never confirmed or denied what was actually taking place. That day, I was reminded one of the first things I learned about reading energy: We're always filtering through the lens of our own experience, so it's good to know what your angle is. That goes for reading someone else's energy, of course, and it's especially helpful when it comes to your own.

So, how do you interpret and decipher the signs that are guiding you? If you pick the "Death" card out of a tarot deck, for example, do you get excited at the opportunity for rebirth or feel sad at the thought of an actual physical death? What about if you feel butterflies in your stomach? Do you take it as excitement about an upcoming opportunity? Or a sign to stay away? And how does that affect your decisions? Your actions? Your intuition? While we can be "voyant" all we want — seeing, feeling, and sensing all around — it's not so useful unless we've got the all-important "clair" part down. In other words, you have to have clear vision if you want to truly see.

So in this chapter, we'll talk about the lens of perception. We'll get into some easy (and even unexpected) ways to identify our blocks to "seeing." And of course we'll talk about ways to clear them — from the physical to the energetical. And while clearing is a life-long journey — in fact, it might be the game of life — this practice not only aids in intuition, but it can transform your path in magical and unexpected ways, often making it easier to manifest what you want. Because what does it mean to see with clarity? It's seeing the truth of who you really are, as a unique human and soul, getting clues about the harmony and love in all things — even an hour-long phone call with your credit card company. Are you ready?

Energetic Filters & Blocks

Energetic filters refer to how we interpret the information we perceive. Sometimes, there are areas in life where we just can't see clearly (yet), and I like to refer to them as smudges on an otherwise clear lens. They're energy blocks, "false" filters, places where we feel resistance, see darkness, experience frustration ...basically, they're ways of perceiving the world that get us stuck, feeling stagnant, or going through sometimes painfully un-fun lessons. They can be the result of stories, beliefs, projections, unexpressed emotions like shame and fear, or simply the result of how our family or culture shaped us that doesn't align with who we really are. And it's helpful to find them, so we know where our blind spots are.

Sometimes, when it feels like your intuition is "off," it may be because you're looking through a false filter. In this case, your intuitive senses may lead you to a clearing experience you need, rather than the experience your conscious self wants. Do you find yourself stuck in the same relationship patterns every time you date? Getting annoyed at co-workers who all seem to push your buttons in exactly the same way, no matter where you work? Injuring the left side of your body over and over? These can all be signs of having smudgy filters, and your intuitive mind trying to clear them for you. And luckily, there are some easy ways to clean them up without having to live out the same stories all the time. First, you have to know how to identify them.

Finding Energy Blocks: Stories, Ideas, Beliefs

The lens through which we're taught to see things is, from a young age, marked by stories and beliefs, gifts and wounds from our past, passed down through our family, culture, and friends. Over the course of our lives, as we carry these imprints, they're often reinforced, rearranged, or altered with experience until we're willing to shed light on the energy beneath them. At this time, we have the opportunity to make a change. But before that, it shapes the way we "see."

I'll give the way too vulnerable example of a belief I used to have that men always leave me. I barely noticed it until I started doing ancestral readings which shed light on the fact that only two generations back — in my grandmother's lifetime — the men were actually forced to leave and go to war, and many of them never came back. And so I'd been acting according to the belief that men don't stick around. The men in my life — even male friends and co-workers — had trouble staying in a room with me for more than a few minutes. It's as if I had a sign stuck to me that said, "Don't hang around this woman longer than 7.5 minutes. Highly volatile. She may explode." And because we all read energy all the time, on some level, I really did have a sign that said that.

To reinforce this energetic imprint, I acted according to this belief, so others would too; I attracted friends who agreed with it, chose to read articles that supported it, and of course I experienced years of it as the belief continued to solidify in my energy field, as if baking a piece of clay to keep its shape. And while none of us humans will ever be perfect, it helps to be aware of these beliefs, especially when they're not the types of experiences we wish to have, nor types of ideas we'd like to spread. And when it comes to reading others? Well, with my clients and out in the world, I double and triple check what I say when I know I have an unclear filter.

So, what's one easy way to clear your filters? First, notice: What patterns repeat themselves over and over again? Is there a sentence people say to you constantly that no one says to your friends? When my friend Garod moved from California to New York and everyone kept asking him, "Why would you come to New York?" he thought it was strange. And it was; when I moved to New York, no one asked me that. When he told me, I suggested it was a question he was wondering himself, holding in his energy field, that it was a filter other people were simply reflecting back at him. He thought for a second and said, "Yeah, you're right. I do think a lot about why I moved here."

What if you notice you're acting according to a filter that doesn't serve you? Remember my old example when I used to count down the minutes before a male human canceled plans on me, cut me off mid-sentence, or ran out of the room entirely? Once you notice your intuition is tuned to predict something you don't actually want, you can ask it instead: What would I rather have happen? And then change the question you ask your subconscious intuitive self to something that's actually useful, such as, Does this man standing in front of me enjoy cooking? Not only does this change your daily experience, your energetic patterning over time, but it also widens the scope of how you read the energy of people, places, and situations by giving you an opportunity to see from new and different angles.

Finding Energy Blocks: Projection

Ever get super mad about something that someone else was doing only to later realize that it's something you do? Yup, me too. When we can't face a quality we don't like in ourselves or really don't want to see, we tend to pin it on everyone else instead. We blindly go around acting according to our stories, ideas, and beliefs, pretty much asking everyone else to fall in line (i.e., *If you're male, please leave me in 7.5 minutes or less)* until we're facing our own stuff dead in the face. So you could say a projection is when we look through a smudgy old filter and see everything in our external world colored by it.

Let's say you're looking through brown sunglass lenses with a scratch over the left eye — the brown color and scratch are going to show up on the people you see, the rooms you find yourself in, even the puppies you pet. I'm sure you can see where I'm going with this: Literally, everything in your world is going to look like s^*t.

The good news is when you notice it — and it's super freaking helpful that our stuff is everywhere so we can — you take what you see on the outside and use it as a helpful hint about what sort of lens you're looking through. Learning to read energy is, of course, a really good way to see your own filters, just as learning about your filters is a good way to refine the way you read energy. And if you don't see your "stuff"? Well, don't worry about that, because your intuition will eventually lead you down a path that makes sure you do.

So, how do you know if you're looking through the lens of projection? If you can't seem to let something go, if there's an emotional charge around it, if you just cannot stand the thought of a bunch of people who seem to be doing something that drives you nuts and yet you end up around the thing that drives you nuts all the time? These are good signs. Which means that if it comes up in life or during an energy reading, you'd better sit quiet for a sec and watch what you're about to say and do. Or...clear it!

Clearing Projections, Ideas, Beliefs & Stories

What's the best thing about noticing your patterns and filters? Once you do, you can work on clearing them, so you can have more of the experiences you want in life! Because, why go through the same annoying lesson out in the world, when you can clear it up at home? And then have more fun in general? Here's one of my favorite and super easy ways to clear ideas, beliefs, projections, and stories next time you notice an uncomfortable pattern come up. This is a simple yet powerful way to heal old wounds, ancestral patterns, even past-life karma and more! Of course, the deeply rooted filters can take some time to clear, but it becomes easier and easier as you make progress on them.

Exercise: Clear Projections, Ideas, Beliefs & Stories

Sit with your eyes closed in meditation. Plug in and center yourself. Then call up the memory of the story or pattern that's causing an issue for you. As you do that, see where you feel sensation in your body. Focus on that sensation and begin to describe it out loud or in a journal.

Example: As soon as I thought of the situation with my co-worker, I felt heat in my right hip. As I concentrated on that warmth, it moved to my left knee where there was a feeling a bit like butterflies, some sadness, then a memory involving my dad from age 5 and this is what happened...

Keep describing for 5 minutes. Not only are you exercising your clair-senses here, but you're focusing your energy on an aspect that needs to be healed. Energy is intelligent, and as you give it loving attention, the pattern will begin to dissolve. As we get into reading ourselves, we'll go even further with this! Until then, use this exercise whenever and wherever needed — you can even take this one to a bathroom stall at work or if you're out with friends and need to do some quick (and so super helpful) clearing.

Finding Energy Blocks: Unexpressed Emotion

Emotions are like passing clouds — they should come and go as quickly as the wind blows. But for some of us, there are times when it feels like the wind hasn't shown up to move those clouds for days. Does this happen to you? If so, it can be a sign of an energy block in the form of holding onto old, unexpressed emotion. Just as your kitchen drain clogs up with bits of gunk that haven't been properly disposed of, our emotional energy body can do the same. And because some of us have been taught to hold back certain emotions — like anger, sadness, jealousy — many of us are still holding on to unexpressed emotions from long ago. Ever have a lump in your throat from holding back tears? If you don't feel that sadness at some point, that clumped-up-ness may stay in your energy body until you do.

Here are some other signs you've got unexpressed emotion clogging your intuitive filters: Do your emotions feel overwhelming at times? Do you sometimes feel others' feelings stronger than your own? Do you often find yourself around overly dramatic people or situations? Do you tend to get more emotionally reactive than a situation actually calls for? Or do you end up stuck in an emotional rut, unable to do anything for days on end? These are all good signs that there are unexpressed or stagnant emotions hanging around. Are you someone who gets frustrated easily? If so, it might be because you have anger you haven't fully expressed.

Our mental and emotional health is crucial to our energetic health and to good intuition. While we've talked about how projections and beliefs color our world, stagnant emotions can fog up our intuitive lenses too. Our emotions want to be felt. And when we feel healthy emotions in present time, they can tell us a lot. On the other hand, if you've cut yourself off from feeling certain emotions in the past, your intuition is probably going to lead you to new situations that will help you feel those feelings — in other words, you'll end up having experiences that will make it pretty hard not to feel. But you know what's more enjoyable than that? Noticing the blocks and clearing old emotions!

Clearing Energy Blocks In The Emotional Body

Many of us have clouded intuition because we were taught to hold back our feelings, or worse, allowed ourselves to be dumped on emotionally or dump on others, which is sort of like dumping trash in a neighbor's yard. The better thing to do is compost it so it doesn't pollute our larger collective. The practice below is one of my favorites for properly disposing of old emotions — in other words, transforming them into wisdom and food for our souls!

I've found that the more I do this, even when I'm not feeling emotional, the more easily emotions come and go, so they don't bowl me over when they shift and change. I do this while shaking out water from my hands after I've washed them. It saves paper, laundry time, and if you're a deep-feeling sensitivista like me, it means being generally less moody all the time! Win, win, win...

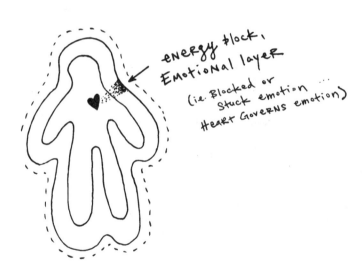

Emotional Energy Clearing, QiGong Style

① LUNG:
color: white
sound: Sssss...

- emotion|s: grief, sadness, inability to let go, stuckness
+ emotion|s: courage, inspiration, ability to let go & transform

③ LIVER:
color: green
sound: Shhh...

- emotion|s: frustration, unhealthy* or unexpressed anger
+ emotion|s: expansion, healthy* anger

② KIDNEY:
color: blue
sound: Choooo.

- emotion|s: fear, limited insight
+ emotion|s: vitality, excitement, wisdom

④ HEART:
color: red
sound: Haaaa....

- emotion|s: resentment, hatred, jealousy, seperation
+ emotion|s: love, compassion, self-compassion, connection

⑤ SPLEEN:
color: yellow
sound: Hooooa...

- emotion|s: worry, stress, anxiety, mistrust
+ emotion|s: trust, self-trust, ease, centered-ness, self-alignment

---

*** healthy vs. unhealthy anger:**
Healthy anger is a feeling that, when felt, can lead to positive action fueled by passion. It also leads to setting healthy boundaries. On the other hand, unhealthy anger or un-felt anger leads to lashing out, reaction, malicious or mis-aligned action. In the chinese tradition, it's said that wood (the element associated with anger) fuels the fire of the heart ♥!

Exercise: *Clear Energy Blocks In The Emotional Body*

This exercise comes from Qigong, which uses physical movement, sound (AKA breath-work), and visualization to clear emotional energy from your physical and subtle body. It emphasizes how every difficult-feeling emotion has a positive polar opposite — like yin and yang — and together, they bring harmony. So it's important to experience both. This helps me know that when I'm feeling sadness, for instance, I can embrace it because it teaches me more about its opposite emotions, like inspiration and courage. The diagram shows a bit about how your physical and emotional body layers work together, each yin/yang or positive/negative emotion, and even the quality of energy (like color or season) associated with it! It might look complicated, but to be honest, it makes the most sense when you just trust it, try it, and experience it for yourself.

STEP 1: Clear Old Emotions from All Energetic Layers by Moving the Body, Making Sound, and Doing Visualization

A. Shake like a maniac. If this feels weird, start with just shaking your hands or make it cute and dance / shake it to your favorite music, and then...

B. Make sound — see the diagram above and start with "SSS".

C. Imagine releasing the color grey into the center of the Earth, composting. (This releases felt memories without us having to recall every story...it's very powerful and soooo easy to do.)

REPEAT. Keep it going while changing the sound to: "CHOO", then "SHHH", "HAA", "WHOAA". The diagram above shows which sound relates to what type of emotion. If this feels silly to you, just make any sound!

STEP 2: Re-Charge Your Energy

Once you've cleared energy and created space, you'll want to fill it with more of the type of energy you want! Refer to the chart and:

A. Face your palms toward your LUNGS and breathe comfortably.

B. Imagine BRIGHT WHITE light shining from your palms into your LUNGS as you remember a time you felt COURAGEOUS. Hold to the count of 10.

REPEAT. Keep going while changing the color, hand position and felt memory to: "BLUE / KIDNEYS / EXCITED", "GREEN / LIVER / EXPANSIVE", "RED / HEART / LOVING & LOVED", "YELLOW / SPLEEN / TRUSTING". The diagram shows what color relates to each type of emotion, and where to position your hands.

Again, this practice comes from Qigong. For those who are unfamiliar, it's sort of like the Taoist or Chinese version of Yoga, with a lot of detailed practices for self-energy healing. The name itself means Energy Practice. In the more advanced version of this practice, each sound is connected to a season and even an element in nature, in addition to an organ system in the body, an emotion, a type of thought…which means that by doing this, we're giving love and respect to each layer of what sustains our body and mind, both internally and externally. In fact, because it's connected to nature, we always start with the *Ssss* sound when releasing because this sound is related to fall, when nature starts to clear! I love this practice because it's detailed and gets at all types of emotional blocks.

Feeling silly about making sounds? Start by making them softly, even imagining at first because…it works! What do we do when we're crying? We make sound. Scared? Sound. This type of release is natural, and not to mention healthy for our bodies. Don't feel comfy shaking like a puppy out of the rain? Try to shake your hands only, put on a song and dance to it, or write out everything you feel and then read it out loud. Using voice moves breath and energy, and that will usually start the tears flowing, which is also a really good way to move old emotional energy.

Finding Energy Blocks:
Stagnant Energy In The Physical Body

Now that you see how your external world can mirror your internal one — that is, holding a specific belief or thought pattern can make it come true — let's look at some of the ways our external world can shed light on our internal filters, by looking at how these things show up physically.

Just like a sieve that's clogged or bent out of shape may not sift flour in certain places, our bodies are the same when it comes to taking in and filtering energetic cues from the outside world. You can think of your body as the physical manifestation of your energetic filters in order to find areas where you're not exactly clear. For example, let's say a boss is hard on you — you may slump one shoulder in order to self-protect. If this happens enough times, your shoulder may keep slumping in order to continue self-protecting, and so the belief that you need to protect yourself gets held in place (along with your aching shoulder).

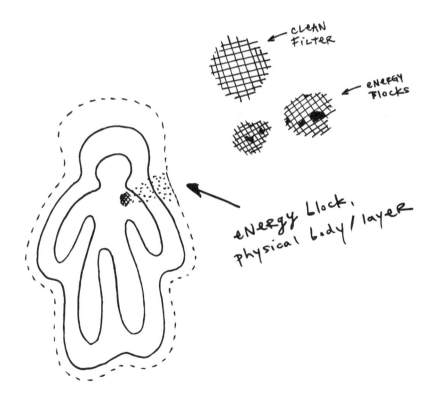

According to one Ayurvedic expert I look up to, muscles and tissues bent out of shape over time develop adhesions and scar tissue, which can block nerve sensitivity over time. So, let's say your shoulder has been slumped over in self-protection mode for a while. Your nerve sensitivity may change. And in that case, it could, for example, mistake the energy of someone who's trying to help you for someone who's trying to harm you. Or, it may not even sense the person trying to help you at all! This doesn't mean your body has to be perfect for good intuition — our bodies are perfect in all their imperfection — but it can give a clue about where your energy blocks are and how to clear your emotional, mental, and of course, physical scars. The body has a miraculous ability to heal itself.

On the flip side, your physical body is a manifestation of your subtle energy body — dissonance starts in the subtle body, then moves its way from outward in. Think of how pretty much everything is made: An object starts off as an idea, a thought form, a pattern of energy, and then someone or something slowly crafts it into being. Even the piece of paper or screen you're looking at right now exists in physical form because someone thought of it. Essentially, it was once just a pattern of energy, and so were you. So, in places your body is experiencing pain, numbness, recurring injury, or imbalance, your energy might simply be "off."

In other words, your body can give a clue as to what's going on emotionally, mentally, or spiritually through metaphor. For example, for a long time, when my right leg started to ache in the presence of a man, I thought I was looking at a man who didn't support women...right side is my masculine, my leg is my support, and only certain men who behaved in certain ways seemed to trigger it. What's more, it was my connective tissue that got injured. Get it? Literally, I had a problem with my connection with certain men. When I noticed it, I worked not just on my injury, but my beliefs and emotions too. And now? I no longer have an issue with an unsupportive leg or the people and situations that mirrored it. What I'm getting at is...one good way to shed light on our energetic patterns is by reading the physical cues. There's often much more there than you think.

Cravings for food, drink, and situations that aren't good for you can also signify there's a "false filter" somewhere in your field. I call it "false" because these are filters that aren't giving us information rooted in loving ourselves or the Earth that sustains us. Would you put sugar in a gas tank that was made to run on fuel? Trash your car that helps you get around? If we want our physical, emotional, and mental body to run well, then we've got to fill it up with what serves it best. This includes healthy ingredients (those you can recognize what type of tree they'd grow on), and ones that were sourced with love and respect for the people and Earth that grew them — for instance, organic, cruelty-free, and local (so not to pollute with gas emissions). Then again, beating up on ourselves for eating ice cream one day isn't loving either — thinking negative thoughts and then feeding ourselves with them is a "false" filter too — but noticing that you're craving a sweet treat from childhood can tell you a lot about what your heart needs, for instance. And when you eat it anyway, you might just want to bless it with the energy of love and whatever else you need.

Curious to know more about your body's signals? There are several systems that can tell you what is out of balance in the physical body and give energetic clues as to why. Chinese and Ayurvedic medicine are two ancient traditions that have been around for centuries and have been written about lots, and on my website you can find links to great resources for both. It also helps to get educated about the ingredients you eat, drink, breathe, use to clean your home, and on your skin (technically your skincare and makeup should be edible) so you're not actively gunking up your own physical, emotional, and mental filters.

Clearing Energy Blocks In The Physical Body

There are so many good options out there for clearing blocks from the physical body; from getting bodywork to internal cleansing, even going for walks in nature to clear stale air from your lungs. And as we get into reading our own energy in the next section, you'll see that even by focusing on an energy block — instead of trying to ignore it or numb it out — can help break up old stagnant energy blocks because our pain is a signal that our body has information for us. And it can actually guide us to a source for healing (just like my headaches led me to this work).

As I mentioned in the last section, part of clearing energy blocks in the body involves watching what you put in your body — just like choosing good fuel for your car. And even if you still crave foods that aren't so good for humans, like sugar, sodas, and chemically processed food, once you start to clean up your diet and physical maintenance regime (remember, skincare and the products you use on your skin and around your home make a big impact too because our lungs and skin absorb what's surrounding us), your body will start to tell you what's good and bad for it. For instance, a client once asked me how to choose the right foods while he was traveling in Asia. Unable to read labels or find out what was in his food, he'd had trouble with his health there before. And so I asked him to try eating only whole foods (that is, foods where you know what tree or plant they grew on) and drinking tons of spring water before the trip. That way, his body would be clear enough that when faced with a bunch of foreign menu options, his intuition would automatically know to choose the best foods for him. Of course, it worked! Remember genetic 1's and 0's from chapter 1? The fact that our bodies are tuned to know what's best for their own survival? Right. And the body can only pick up these signals if it has clear filters. The "Yes/No" Exercise in Chapter 2 is super helpful for tapping into this innate skill.

When chronic illnesses and injuries present themselves, you can start to clear them by getting curious about their root cause — journaling about it is a good starting point, and it may lead you to the right healing method for you, which could be anything from getting more exercise to taking naps. Or, when you're clear, you might suddenly remember the name of the perfect healing method or practitioner you wanted to try. You may even notice that as physical blocks are worked out of the body, emotions and memories of childhood wounds come up and out of your field, like bubbles coming up to the surface of water to be released.

While there are soooo many options for different healing modalities, here's a really easy practice you can do anytime, anywhere. It helps to clear old bits of stuck energy, clear old trauma from the body, release muscle tension, allow new energy to flow and circulate through you, and more! And it's just so easy...

Exercise: Clear Energy Blocks In The Physical Body

My favorite exercise for clearing stagnant energy from the body is simple: Put on your favorite song and dance like a maniac. Playing a song that sounds good to you is soothing to your soul, AND your body always knows intuitively how to move in order to release the right places. Really, this one's too easy not to do. :)

Don't like to dance? Not a fan of music? Set a timer and shake. All you have to do is shake your body. Start with 2 minutes per day and work up to 12. If that feels silly, start by just shaking your hands.

*FUN FACT: Energy clearing out of the physical body can sometimes feel like bubbles bursting, twitches, waves of heat releasing, laughing, crying, silly sound making, even burping, belching, passing gas, sneezing, coughing, yawning and more! And following these, there is usually a huge burst of vital energy.

PS. It's possible that during or just before a big clearing, you will experience whatever you were holding onto big-time. It might feel surreal or even difficult. If so, take care of your physical body by eating healthy food, drinking lots of water, getting plenty of rest, meditation and exercise, and seeking the advice of a professional if needed.

Finding Energy Blocks:
Stagnant Energy In Your Living Space

I am always amazed at how my physical space reflects what's going on in my personal one. Seriously, there've been times in my life where it was as if my flickering lamp or leaky faucet was telling me where I was leaking my power away. One time I wondered why my friends weren't coming over to my new place, until I realized I was living behind a solid brick wall that was opposing the entrance to my home.

Our space has a lot to tell us about the way we filter energy, which is cool because then the opposite is true too — reorganize your space, set new intentions, and your filters change with it. Do you feel welcome in a really messy space? Clear-headed in a room that's cluttered or noisy with bad smells? It's harder to think than, say, being in a harmonious spot in nature. Having trouble getting over your ex but have her stuff still in your drawers? Unsure about why you're experiencing an intuitive block? Clean up and clear out your space and see if it sheds any light. I often find if I'm having trouble with intuition, all I have to do is spend an hour cleaning, and new insights begin to flow, along with the fresh energy. There are also some great traditions that can tell us about how our space translates to our personal life and energy. The ancient Chinese art of Feng Shui is one of my favorites.

Clearing Energy Blocks In Your Living Space

This one's an easy fix: Clean, organize, donate, repair, or re-purpose things that no longer represent who you are or want to be. Then, think about things like: How's the air in your house? The light? Are there cords everywhere? Relics of situations you'd rather forget? Dead things that used to be living? Things that haven't moved for awhile? Seemingly unmovable obstacles? Cracks in objects that offer support? Singles of everything, even though you'd rather be part of a pair? What's the first thing someone will see and therefore know about you when they enter your space? What's the first thing you see that will act as your inspiration every day? I have a mood board in front of my bed as the first thing I see when I wake up, and because I love nature, I make sure I always live near trees.

To get a good idea of how energy moves through your space, imagine it filled with water and notice where it's likely to get trapped in certain places. My super-sensitive sister Cristalle arranges things from tallest to shortest. You can get yourself a good Feng Shui book if you want to follow a detailed traditional method, or just take stock of what's around and what your things mean to you. Once you clear your space, you're in a good spot to call in what you really want. For instance, I once bought a plant and called him Stevie, put him in my career-themed corner to call in more joy in that area of my life, and attracted a hilarious business partner by the same name.

While clearing out is helpful, you can also choose to change the lens you look through at the objects you wish to keep — giving the things you love (or must keep) a new meaning. For instance, I can decide my wall is there to protect and keep me safe. That a gift from an ex is an ode to getting over heartbreak and previously held beliefs about what it means to love. If you have things that feel awkward, like a crack in the wall of your rental, don't sweat it, just give it a fresh intention and update it as best you can — decorate it, enliven the area with a plant, or love it up in some other fun and creative way like making a mural to cover it with your friends, so when you look at the crack, it reminds you of your community. That way, you're programming the energy of your things, your physical filters, so they're in line with what you want.

Exercise: Clear Energy Blocks In Your Living Space

To energetically clear objects and space, try one of these ideas!

- Put out a bowl of water in the center of your space. Just as water dissolves physical matter, it breaks down energy too.

- Re-energize objects by putting them outside in a cycle of sun and moon light for 72 hours.

- Energetically cleanse objects by burying them in sea salt for 72 hours.

- Use crystals, plants, or other objects from nature to bring the frequencies of Mother Nature indoors.

- Use a smudge with a specific intention in mind. Make sure to open windows so the smoke and old energy clears out! It's nice to use something local or that has a smell you like. Some good smudges are: Sage for cleansing, Palo Santo for uplifting, Cedar for clearing confusion and bringing wisdom, Frankincense for enhancing third eye intuition. Of course, we can see smoke filling the space of even the hardest-to-reach corners, and it represents burning up the old, but if it bothers your lungs, try an essential oil diffuser or spray; Rosewater is lovely for enlivening the heart, and you can even light candles to call in the energy of fire!

- Clear space by using harmonious sound — singing bowls, tuning forks, chimes, voice or even a favorite song that represents the vibe you want to call in!

- Give your space a Neutral Grounding Cord and imagine sucking energy from all corners of the room toward it like a vacuum. Send the old energy down to the center of the Earth to compost it. Then imagine gold neutral sparkly energy or even a pleasant sound or fragrance to recharge it! (This works for any room you find yourself in, by the way.)

- Speak out loud a new intention for your space, welcoming the energy you want to be around — sound carries vibration.

Or work with energy by giving the room its own Grounding Cord and imagining that bits of old stagnant energy from each corner of the room are being sucked into the center of the room, then down into the Earth for composting. You can even give it an energetic reset by visualizing gold neutral energy filling the space when you're done, or give it a pleasant sound or smell in your mind's eye. This even works for public spaces! (And for your own personal auric space too.)

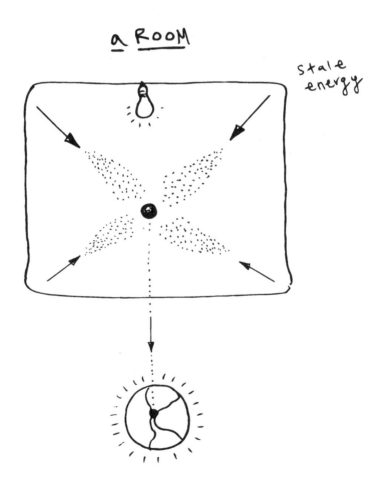

Leaving Your Body

Just like leaving your physical space with the door wide open may invite in unexpected visitors, same goes for leaving your energetic space or trying to have an "out of body" experience. When you're not fully aligned or present in your body, it leaves you open to making intuitive decisions that serve someone else, some other thing or time and place — wherever your energy, focus, or thoughts may be.

Having a pleasant inner body experience, on the other hand, can be much more fulfilling than being out of yourself, so you can fulfill your own individual path and needs. Healing your physical and energetic injuries can make being in your body more enjoyable, so you can have the full scope of experience, with your inner and outer worlds in harmony. And since I'm someone who easily leaves my body, I know that getting back in can be a journey, but as I worked on it, I noticed the more voice I gave to my vastly rich energetic experience, the more it integrated with my physical one.

It's also worth mentioning that sometimes our subtle energetic space is not "clear" because we've decided to "give" or "take" energy from another person or group of people — kind of like letting someone else live in our space. Often, there are pure intentions, for instance, you're wanting to help a friend or you've been taught you need to share your space — but it's not always useful to you or the other person if you're mixing energies long term. We'll talk more about detangling energies in a little.

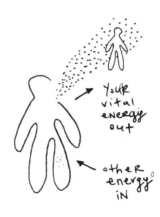

Reclaiming Your Own Energy

There are so many reasons we subconsciously choose to leave our bodies, or our energetic space, and knowing about them helps us get back to where we want to be — in our bodies. Maybe you're curious and like to go out and explore, or maybe your space just feels too messed up, clogged with stagnant energy, and you're looking for somewhere cleaner to hang out. But again, leaving your body open to others' energy, opinions, and intuition could mean losing clear sight of your own. Nonetheless, there will be times when we lose ourselves, and it's good to have tools for clearing out and coming back in.

To reclaim your energetic space, it can help to reclaim your physical body first. You can do this by using the exercises above (maniacal dancing or shaking is always fun) or by using some other simple tools like taking a shower or salt bath, walking in nature, or doing something you love that reminds you of who you are, even calling a friend. Sometimes, after a heavy reading or emotional experience with another person, I'll dance or shake to some music with heavy bass (think root chakra, lower energy centers, connection to Earth), do jumping jacks, or talk to myself in the mirror — all things that help me come back to myself.

Calling Back Your Energy

Once you've cleared energy from the body, it's typical to want to fill that empty space with something — and we have a tendency to replace it with more of the same. But for best results, sit and feel that newly created space, then fill it with your own neutral essence. The tool below is one for calling back your own energy, which we'll revisit again and again. In fact, once we get to readings, this is how you'll close them. Really, this is so helpful after any clearing — energy readings are often also clearings — and you can use it daily as needed. I find this one especially useful before a presentation or after a social media binge! This is also a great one for those who help and heal others.

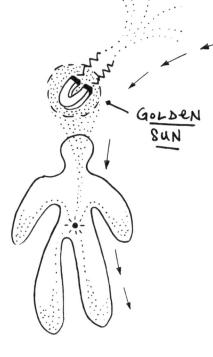

ENERGY TOOL #2:
Calling Back Your Energy

To Open: Set Intentions

Speak out loud or write out your intention for the clearing; e.g., to separate from someone* or something you may have merged with, or to simply feel more aligned in the present moment. I like to call in Archangels Michael, Metatron, Raphael, Gabriel, or another higher source of guidance I'm resonating with for help with any ritual, reading, or energy work — I recommend trying it if it speaks to you.

*Separating, breaking ties, detangling, un-merging energies with someone — or however you want to refer to it — doesn't mean severing the relationship. It just means cleaning it up, like clearing your cache or hitting the reset button, so you can experience a fresh, clean relationship where each of you can stand in your own most powerful space and sense of alignment.

STEP 1: Plug in Your Energy

Yup, Energy Tool #1. Plug in your energy: Run your Earth, Cosmic, and Neutral Grounding Cord to align and balance. This clears and refreshes your energy by connecting to a greater energy field. And if you've been practicing, it should be super quick and easy by now!

STEP 2: Gather up Scattered Bits of Energy

C. Hold your arms above your head and/or visualize a golden ball of light there. Working with the color gold will help to neutralize any energy coming back to you.

D. Visualize a magnet in the center of it and write your name on it or, if you more clairsentient, feel the energy between the palms of your hands.

If you can't feel the energy now, you will with practice. It's very subtle. To me, it feels dense and magnetic, while others describe it as spongy. If you can sense it, describe out loud. How does it feel to you?

E. Announce that you're calling back your own energy from all corners of the Earth, and be specific. For example, call your energy back from your phone and other devices, from your work, your partner, family and friends, all the places you've been, an emotional situation, a pet, a past wound, etc. No one will be hurt by you calling your own energy back — in fact, it's best for everyone if we've all got our own energy running in our own space. See, feel or sense the ball above your head getting bigger and more dense.

STEP 3: Bring in Your Energy

Bring it down over your body from up above your head and all the way down to cover the area below your feet, so your aura feels filled up with YOU.

To Close: Feel Your Own Energy

Sit for a minute, feeling your own energy running.

...Then, journal! Describe it, in detail, on the next page. What's your signature color? Texture? Scent? Defining its material world qualities will make it easy to call it back anytime you need! For example, your energy could be peach colored, with a soft watery texture, and smell like roses. Yum! :)

write:

_____
_____
_____
_____

color in!

Uncovering Your Hidden Gems

At this point, I'll acknowledge this may seem like a lot of things, but we're human, after all, and we've all got our filters — from cultural beliefs (such as having the most money is important) to experiences that are totally and completely our own. It's why I can say a word with one intention, and you may take it to mean something different entirely. It's what makes each of us unique, and that's a beautiful thing. But what if you feel like you've got super gunked-up filters? Well, I know from experience there are times in life when it feels like all you're doing is clearing endless amounts of smudge from your filters. But thankfully there are so many easy (and sometimes entertaining) ways to release this stuff. Personally, I'm all about the experiences in life, so I've done all sorts of things from having clarified butter poured in my eyes (an ancient Ayurvedic practice that involves wearing dough goggles — yes, like the stuff you use for baking) — to letting a Tao Master shoot at my heart with an invisible ray of love... which felt like butterflies, by the way. And then there are those easy everyday energetic maintenance sorts of things that, if you keep at it and have faith, can lead you to uncover your own special inner gems.

Claiming Your Superpowers!

5.

Spiros In Spirit

It started on a Monday with a craving for tzatziki. By Wednesday, I noticed myself talking Greek wine with a friend. By Thursday, three people asked me if I did mediumship readings — to which I replied, "Who me? No... totally normal psychic stuff over here." And on Friday, when my old Greek friend Petros reached out to ask if I could connect him with a friend who'd passed on, well, I tried to ignore it. Because growing up in a culture that labeled this sort of thing as paranormal meant I rarely told anyone it was something I could do. On one hand, I was terrified to admit my shameful secret; on the other, it hurt my heart not to help a friend.

The next day I woke up and asked for guidance. And that's when I checked my phone and saw that the last message from Petros had something strange in it. Between the lines of the text I'd sent him the night before, it said in big red letters, about five times: BOOK APPT. I laughed out loud, and finally, I caved. I guess what we could call a magical tech glitch happened at exactly the right time. So thank you, Spiros — of course this spirit's name actually looks like it should be the Greek word for spirit — if that was you, then I'm still impressed by your genius.

After the reading, I was in awe. Not only was it something of a "coming out" for me that touched my heart in ways I can't even express, but the reading was so beautiful, so powerful, the message that came through and the reuniting of friends so profound, it felt like I was high for days after...until I realized Spiros had moved in with me. And with my new roommate, my old feelings of fear around this stuff too. I kept trying to release the reading, asking him to go, but as soon as it seemed like he was gone, he come back in. I'd find myself cooking Greek food, leaving blue and white things everywhere, including a shirt that looked like the flag of Greece I never even wear. It was funny for a second, until it wasn't. I don't see spirits with my physical eyes, but I sure do feel their presence, and his was big and hanging around. I panicked.

Ashamed of my gift once again, my curious and inviting nature, I asked him to leave through tears. "Come on, Spiros, you have to go...NOW!" I screamed, but when my lights flicked on and off, I started laughing. Because he was right on with that cute metaphor — we were kind of in an on-again, off-again type of relationship. Which I hadn't even thought about until I called my teacher Debra, frantic, and she asked bluntly, "Well, are you sure you really want him to leave?" I couldn't say that I did. And that's when I realized he'd stayed because deep down, I'd wanted him to. I was so touched by the reading that I was the one choosing to keep up the connection. And when I was finally able to admit that, I was also able to choose to let him go.

So why this random ghost story before we get into reading energy? First off, because maybe you, like me, used to try to pretend — even to yourself — that you don't believe in these types of experiences. Second, because there seems to be some fear around this stuff and I wanted to highlight the fact that you always have a choice about who — and what — to interact with. Third, when you feel like you don't, it's often because of parts of yourself you don't want to face — like the part of me that didn't want to admit I talk to spirits, for instance. Or that I enjoy it. And fourth, when you do open up to your scary, shadowy, dark parts, they can turn out to be beautifully heartwarming, even entertaining, and help you claim more of your personal power that was just waiting for you to uncover it. So, in this chapter, we're going to do some more clearing by talking about entangled energies, boundaries, and the importance of darkness and light.

☯ Yin & Yang: Shadow & Light

Let's talk yin and yang, the principle of shadow and light, the formless and the formed, feminine and masculine, cold and hot, moon and sun, everything and its perfect opposite... polarity. It's pretty much the lesson of this great Earth. And what do you get when two opposing forces are perfectly aligned? Like equal weights on a scale, you get balance, neutrality, harmony. If you look at a yin-yang symbol, there are two equal pieces, with light in darkness and darkness within light. Together, all parts create a whole harmonious circle. Kind of like this Earth school. So while we can "love and light" all we want, unless we honor the darkness, we're missing something. Like, half of the whole experience, actually.

Let's take, for example, one of the scariest, darkest things most of us humans can think of: Death. Yup, I went there. Because I want to talk about the fact that nothing, absolutely nothing is black and white, but very much grey. In fact, I wrote this during one of the darkest times I've ever had, and it was yet another super dark period that led up to rediscovering my passion for writing. And with it, my passion for life.

I was living in New York City with a cool job in fashion photography. I had no time to make art like I used to. I wasn't taking any photos or doing anything creative at all. I'd wake up, go to work, exercise, come home...eat, sleep, work, repeat. My life was on autopilot and I was so used to it that I barely noticed time just passing me by. That is, until the day my friend died. A successful fashionista herself, she worked hard all her life to afford a pretty Park Avenue apartment, a wardrobe full of beautiful clothes, and other very covetable things. But she was miserable. And when we lost her to cancer, I was the one left clearing out her apartment, cleaning up after her life.

One Saturday, I was sitting on the floor of her beautiful apartment alone, trying to sort through her closet. I'd taken out all her stuff — shoes, bags, dresses — and found myself buried in a pile of everything I'd ever dreamed of owning, when I noticed that absolutely none of it was bringing me any joy. I felt empty, depleted, curious about the fact that I'd spent years of my life doing things I only sort of loved just so I could survive. And when that didn't bring happiness, I worked harder at it, did more of it, so I could buy more things to uplift my mood a little while working so hard to stay afloat. But none of it could make that empty feeling go away. Because here I was surrounded by all these things, still miserable, tired. And as I sat there, I realized that *that* felt kind of like death.

It was at that moment I decided I wanted to actually live. Sitting on that floor, I decided to quit my career-life — a scary and super dark idea for someone who comes from immigrant parents and started working at the age of 15. I decided to return to what I love doing, as much as possible — I started making art again and spending time with people who make my heart sing. Being surrounded by death, I learned what it was to live. And it opened my eyes to see there are treasures buried in every experience, messages hiding in the dark, especially when you agree to face the pain.

And while we're on the subject of pain, I have to mention that it was the same with my once chronic illness. Had I never had crazy headaches, I would have never discovered the gift of my own sensitivity. And a health crisis certainly seems like a dark and painful event, doesn't it? But once I realized that my chronic migraines were a direct result of my extremely active third eye, my heightened intuitive abilities, and started learning all about energy...well, do you think the situation is all bad? Dark? Toxic? Not in the slightest. Yes, it was once difficult to lie in bed for days, unable to feel my own face, and even more so, not to know how to talk about it, but I wouldn't trade that experience now for anything because it led me to uncover one of my most cherished gifts. And what's more, it helped me develop compassion for my oh-so-lovable, super sensitive body, to learn to listen when it tells me that sometimes — headache or no — I really just need to stay in bed. That's just me. And I love it.

Darkness really does have the power to illuminate us in profound and magical ways — if we're open to seeing it that way. If we push away darkness, we miss understanding the profound beauty of a whole picture. And that means we're blind to the lesson of love buried underneath the tough stuff. So, darkness can contain messages of love as much as light does — just think of the magic of a shooting star in an otherwise dark night sky. Of course, I choose not to use either dark or light energy as a vice, and I use discernment when choosing which energies to engage with and ask that my lessons come through pleasurable situations as much as possible, please. But the point is, I no longer look away from what only at first seems to be dark.

EVERYTHING IS YIN & YANG!

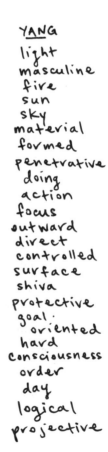

Yin	Yang
dark	light
feminine	masculine
water	fire
moon	sun
earth	sky
ethereal	material
formless	formed
receptive	penetrative
being	doing
rest	action
flow	focus
inward	outward
subtle	direct
spontaneous	controlled
deep	surface
shakti	shiva
nurturing	protective
process-oriented	goal-oriented
soft	hard
life-force	consciousness
chaos	order
night	day
intuitive	logical
reflective	projective

Shadows & Blind Spots

I'm going to assume you know about light, but let's talk about shadows. These are the not-so-savory parts of ourselves we often don't want to look at. While other people can usually see exactly what they are, if we don't make a conscious effort to look, they can go unnoticed — like blind spots. So, if in Chapter 4 we said that filters refer to how we perceive the world, here I'll say that shadows are the lies we tell ourselves to justify keeping our "false" filters in place. And that muddies up our intuition. So, here we're going to work on loosening them up a little so we can clear our filters even more and align a little deeper with ourselves.

Take, for example, the denial of my mediumship abilities. I see now that I must've thought seeing and talking to spirits and ghosts was weird, and so I literally could not admit any of it — even to myself. As a result, I was blind to all of it. One way I shut down my gifts was by unconsciously giving myself headaches — putting myself out of commission for days when I started to perceive things. If someone talked about psychic or medium stuff, I might've bolted out of the room or stopped talking to that person altogether, without giving much thought as to why. And who knows what else I did? In a sense, you could say I was once blind to the gifts that now allow me to see.

Each of us carries shadows and blind spots we're meant to illuminate along our path — life wouldn't be an adventure without them. I like to think of these shadows and blind spots as places we don't perceive love in yet, as smudges over the perception of an otherwise clear lens. You can choose to see around your smudgy lenses or you can work with them, just like we did with clearing filters. And you can do this simply by agreeing to look at them, love them, and decide you're not afraid. As we talked about in the last chapter, by being aware of the smudges, even if only for a minute, you can attune your vision to the truth of what's fully there.

In life, this means suddenly being able to see, do, change, create or manifest what you never thought possible. Why? Because you're no longer wasting precious energy holding back a part of yourself. By being open to darkness as much as light, yin as much as yang, both sides of yourself, you open to seeing the full spectrum of your personal power. And I believe that the Life-Force, or whatever you want to call it, really doesn't make mistakes with how we were made. So, why not love all your parts?

Because darkness makes up half of our whole selves, it's super important we honor the fact it exists. Or at least admit that it does. And if we don't? Well, in my experience, if we don't want to believe in darkness, then we literally can't see it until it smacks us in the face. And whoa, when that happens, does it hurt. Take, for instance, control dynamics in relationships. We'll talk more about this in a bit, but oh was this once a painful lesson for me. Ever met a guy or girl so charming you'd literally do anything they'd say, even if you knew it wasn't good for you? Out of alignment with who you are at your very core? And you let them tell you things even though you knew they were kidding themselves — and you — just so you wouldn't have to point it out? Right. And I used to think it was all that person's fault for being all-powerful over a weak little sensitivista like me who must have looked like prey to their narcissistic overpowering ways. Until I learned that deciding I was a victim was just my shadow talking. And I was attracting people like this, practically begging them to treat me this way to illuminate what I couldn't see: that I'd decided I was weak. So as it turned out, situations like these were literally the best lessons in personal power I ever could have asked for. Because to get out of this pattern, I had to prove to myself I was strong. What originally looked like a dark cloud had a very silver lining.

Entities

So why am I talking power dynamics? Because we have to talk about the idea that there are things lurking in the shadows that can overpower us, energies we must protect ourselves from. To me, entities, "dark" energies, shadows, and heavy belief systems are all one and the same, in that can they sap our power — but only if we are afraid to "see" them. And the belief that these are energies we must be fearful of...well, to me, this looks like yet another example of choosing to give our power away. Fear of darkness and dark beings is a harmful belief because it means believing we have decided we're not powerful enough to make our own choices. It's a bit of a cop-out, really. On the other hand, if we understand the darkness, at least acknowledge its presence, it gives us the power to choose how to engage with it.

Take, for example, Spiros, my cheeky little ghost friend. At first I thought he was haunting me, but then I realized I'd asked him to stay, for my own benefit. One could say that a formless being is "dark." I mean, just tell your most conservative-minded friend you're going to start talking to ghosts and see what she has to say. But Spiros was hilarious! I wouldn't trade the time I had with him for anything. And had I not let him into my home and heard what he had to say, I never would have received the many gifts that came from the experience: helping a friend, welcoming my gifts, my personal power, and even a silly story. And yes, if you're super sensitive like me, you might've actually seen a creepy-feeling dark spot of energy running across the floor, but like a mouse or a bug you don't want in your room, why not just choose to see them and direct them outside?

I've witnessed dissonant energy showing up in different ways: sometimes as a dark, little blob in a room or on a person, a random and unexplainable cold spot or cool breeze, an uncontrollable twitch in my body that feels like it's trying to ward something away, an unpleasant smell or taste, a note played out of tune, you name it. And while I was once naturally afraid of what was never explained to me — what my parents seemingly couldn't protect me from because they didn't see what I could — I've now come to accept these things. And as I accept the existence of shadows, in them I can see light — if I choose to engage, that is. Because much like people I choose not to hang around, I understand that I don't have to hang out with any shadows or heavy belief systems I don't want to, and so the thought of them no longer makes me afraid.

For the sake of illuminating this topic even more, I'll say I've seen "dark" spots appear when I focus on negative words, beliefs, unresolved shadow aspects and trauma. And I've seen these bits float away when someone has an enlightening realization about one or more of these things. And I've noticed these spots of darkness show up more often when talking about heavy beliefs that many people carry. For instance, the belief that men always earn more than women — to me, that thought pattern looks like an entity. Another one? That certain people can be toxic or bad. What is toxic or bad is the belief all humans and situations weren't created perfectly, and that we don't have the power to choose or change our experience. Because that is what saps our power — the fear of powerlessness, of darkness itself. So, taking our personal power back means simply deciding that we have choices when it comes to shadow and darkness.

In the example with the "narcissists," it was the belief that they — or anyone, really — had power over my choices that was harmful to me. And since power dynamics in relationships (even human-shadow ones) teach us lessons in power, the second we decide to claim our personal power, it means we no longer have to engage in uncomfy relationships in order to learn these lessons. An easy option? Say to yourself, "You know, this thought about _____ is freaking me out and I really don't feel like hanging out with this right now. I see it, though." A mentor once told me it's like the choice between noticing there are cars zooming past vs. jumping in front of them and getting in. In other words, choose wisely. And we'll go deeper into energy give-and-take dynamics in a sec. But first, a little exorcise...

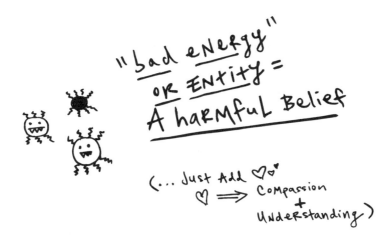

Ex-orcise: Shadow & Light

Let's face it, sometimes it can feel heavy and scary to move through our shadows and the dark times that exist as a result of them. Sometimes experiencing them fully (without acting them out on anyone else) is the only way to see the light. Next time you're feeling the darkness, try this…

Write about a time you felt truly unconditionally loved and held by a friend, family member, spiritual guide, or even a pet. Then read it out loud and notice the shift in your vibration. Can you suddenly see the light side of the dark situation? Can you be open to knowing you'll understand it later? Can you feel one step closer to seeing the whole picture? How does your body feel?

When I'm feeling dark, I go to my altar, where I've put all the objects I've collected over the years that brought me uplifting messages or expressions of love from friends. There are coins that carried messages I asked for, heart-shaped rocks that bumped up against my feet during times I've needed love, mementos from friends who support me and wish me well. Any time I'm in the dark, I have a place to go that takes me back to love, reminding me that soon I'll see the light. For that, I'm grateful.

"Taking On" & "Giving Away" Energy

When we get into the realm of energy, giving and taking seems to be a big question, as in, How do you break the pattern of entanglement, like from taking, giving, or inviting invasive-feeling energy? While it might seem scary, especially for us sensitive souls (and those who've watched creepy movies), it's simple to understand. As was the case with the hilarious ghost of Spiros, we have to ask ourselves why we're agreeing to the exchange. Often, it's linked to an exciting memory we don't want to let go of, or the fear of not being able to survive without the energetic pattern we're choosing to attach to.

Habits of giving and taking energy are usually based on patterns we picked up as kids, when we were learning how to survive in the world. After all, kids don't have what it takes to survive on their own and therefore must rely on their families and communities for safety. Kids are also super perceivers of energy. While we adults have to meditate or work at conscious dreaming to put our brainwaves into Theta or Alpha state (the energy perceiving state), kids have been shown to live full-time in Theta state until around age 7. My mother always said I could "see" through walls as a child, and said she thought I'd make a good interior designer. Well, she was close! But seriously, since kids are expert workers of energy, they'll give to a parent who doesn't seem to be well enough to take care of them, or they'll take from a parent who has a need to over-give. Which side of the spectrum do you fall on? Do you ever give or take because, on some level, you feel you have to?

And why does this throw off intuition? Because if you're in the mode of give or take, you're attuned to the needs of another person, rather than your own. And your intuition will respond that way — by serving the other person or shutting down altogether. And as you see, it can come from an innocent or unconscious place. But by being aware of your patterns, you don't have to be afraid of them or stuck in them, and you can easily choose to make shifts. Of course, there's nothing wrong with giving and taking — humans are interdependent creatures — but you just want to make sure that if you are exchanging energy, you're doing it from a place of love rather than fear, for best results.

So how do you stop giving or taking energy if it's a problem for you? I can only speak to those who over-give, because that's what I learned to do. Here's what stopped it for good: I learned that when I helped someone without their asking me to, or rescued them too much, I was actually hurting them because I'd robbed them of a lesson they needed to learn. So, in a sense, I wasn't just over-giving, but taking more than my fair share of lessons. Not cool. But the first step for changing any energetic pattern is simply to notice — to illuminate what was once in the shadows.

And what if you're just worrying about someone? Mixing energies with the intention of showing you care? When you worry about someone, you're energetically sending the message, "Hey, I don't think you can handle this on your own." And you know what ends up happening? They feel you don't have faith in them, and it only gets you more tangled up. But when you truly have faith in someone, you're energetically saying, "I love you just as you are, and I believe in you." Then they'll feel an energy ripple of strength and empowerment. Not only does it make for cleaner energy exchanges, but it sends a message to the Universe that you trust in your own path, your own life lessons and theirs. It's not always easy, but it's so impactful when you try it out! If you struggle with worrying about others, try making that sentence into a mantra and see how powerful it really is!

But, while this stuff makes sense in theory, sometimes it can get us sensitives down. Personally, I've really struggled with this stuff, and so do many of the sensitive people I meet. There's no better healer training than if we've had to do this from birth, right? It takes a while to shift sometimes. But it's worth noting that even some of the most senior healers I've studied with admit they sometimes give or take energy. The best advice I've received is to let it blow past like a gust of wind. Or walk away to reset. Think of trying to block wind with a parachute — after awhile it gets heavy to hold. But if you work with it, let it be, even enjoy how it feels, it will eventually die down. In other words, trying to push energy away or resist it only makes it feel heavy. Acceptance is the only way — fear and shame over it only stagnates the energy, so you're stuck holding that heavy, wind-filled parachute in place. Basically, most helpful is simply to shed light on these energetic patterns so they don't throw you off. And so...

Exercise: Shedding Light On Energy "Give" and "Take"

You may already be familiar with some places you tend to give and take energy, others not so much. Usually when these patterns come up, your mood changes suddenly, your body feels heavy or drained, you're agitated or anxious, you might lose touch with your intuition. We all have these patterns, and knowing when they tend to happen starts to shift them over time. So first, ask yourself whether it feels more familiar to give or take. Here are some questions to get the juices flowing: Do you feel more comfortable giving a gift or getting one? Giving advice or taking some? Helping someone or being helped? Write your answer here:_____.

And no shame! We all give and take. If your pattern feels out of balance, though, try acting out the other side for a little while to balance out. We'll talk more about this at the end of the exercise. Moving on...

STEP 1: Identifying Stories — Energy Give & Take

Here, we're going to shed light on some of the stories that come up for you around giving or taking energy, how it feels in your body (e.g., draining, heavy, tense) and what types of emotions (e.g., anxious, annoyed, angry) you feel so you can better recognize when this stuff crops up.

A. Think of a recent situation that left you feeling drained of energy, heavy, overly emotional maybe. Who was there? What type of relationship do you have with that person? What happened? Write about it:

_____
_____
_____
_____

B. At what point did you begin to feel drained, heavy, tense, emotional, at a loss for words even? What did you do? Write about it:

_____
_____
_____
_____
_____

C. Has something like that happened before? If so, when? And with whom? Who do they remind you of? And why? Write about it:

_____
_____
_____
_____
_____

STEP 2: **Identifying Stories — Losing Touch With Your Center**

Often, when we're stuck in a pattern of energy give or take, we end up losing touch with our center. This can mean following someone else's intuition instead of your own, or being unable to hear your inner guidance. So...

A. Write about a situation that happened recently when you felt like you acted or spoke in a way that wasn't in your best interest and, in a sense, followed someone else's intuition or path. Who was there? What type of relationship do you have with that person? Who do they remind you of? What happened? Did you feel drained? Heavy? Did your emotions change? Body language shift? Did your voice get louder or softer, or did you find yourself using language that doesn't even sound like you? Write about it on the next page.

_____
_____
_____
_____
_____

B. Has something like that happened before? If so, when? And with whom? Who do they remind you of? And why? Write about it:

_____
_____
_____
_____
_____

If you feel emotional after this exercise, that's normal. In fact, it's even welcome because it means you found a juicy bit of shadow. To move it out of your energy field, sit and feel your feelings for at least 5 minutes — longer if you have time. It's best to do this until the wave of emotion dissolves. It's sometimes hard, but afterwards you'll feel lighter and more clear. To finish up, use Energy Tools #1 and #2 to reset your energy and come back to center. Then, if you feel it, write a bit of encouragement for yourself here, since recognizing our patterns takes strength and humility, and it means we have the power to change them!

_____
_____
_____
_____
_____

And Now A Bit On Boundaries

This feels like a good place to talk boundaries, since we're talking energy give and take, and because soon we're going to start playing with energy. Because if we're literally going to go poking around in someone else's field — with permission, of course — we've got to have a good understanding of how to feel good when we do. So we have to have strong boundaries in place, and at the same time loosen up a bit on our boundaries. That's right: The question of boundaries is a funny one — it's something you want to focus on and yet not focus on too much. And it's often a biiiiig topic for those of us who sense a lot. And honestly, it's even a big one for those who don't, because it could be one of the reasons *why* you're not sensing much at all. Or it could even be one of the reasons why others aren't sensing you. Many of us have been taught, indirectly and mostly through cultural programming, to put up something of a wall. For safety, we've been told.

So what happens when you've got a big impenetrable wall up around your energy space? Well, it might be hard for others to come in. Which could be a good thing, depending on what you want or don't want to experience. But you know what else? It's also not so easy to get out. And energetically, this translates to energetic "junk" building up inside the walls of your own personal energy space. Nothing in, nothing out. Not even the sound of your own voice. Having trouble being heard? Being seen for who you are? That's a good sign to check in on your energetic boundaries, which you can do simply by sensing them, or reading yourself (which we'll get to soon) while deciding to take a look at the space immediately around you. Like checking out the structure of a fence built around your home.

What about having no boundaries at all? Or a big hole in your energetic fence down low by the ground so that anything small and creepy crawly can get in? This is something you want to look for too. And it's surprisingly easy to mend any holes or too-big spaces in your boundaries if you notice they're there. How? First, by taking a look at what's there. Second, by deciding you want to change them and imagining having more ideal boundaries. Sounds too easy, I know. But try playing with it and notice how much starts to shift around you. Soon, we'll get into an energy tool for maintaining ideal boundaries. First, a lil' diagram...

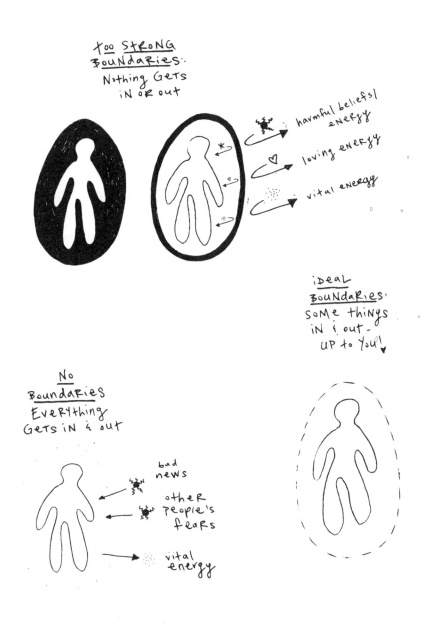

As you can see, the ideal boundaries are the ones that let some stuff in and keep other stuff out. The ones that give you a personal choice. Often, feeling energetic overwhelm and the anxiety that comes along with it can be attributed to either having weak boundaries (sensing everything), having too-thick boundaries (holding in too much "stuff"), or putting too much emphasis on your boundaries to the point it feels like you're **trying** to hold up an energetic shield all day long and your arms are getting tired. **Ever feel** super drained after a situation you weren't sure you wanted to be in? **That was** you focusing too much on trying to hold up your shield. Instead, we want to pour a little more grace on it.

Remember, if like **attracts** like in energy, and you're afraid of something scary, you will most likely find **yourself** near something to be scared of; and if you feel you need to protect yourself, you'll attract things you need to be protected from. If you overly focus on **boundaries**, you create something of an energetic wall, meaning it's hard to be **properly** seen or heard, and, of course, you're going to meet other walled-off people, or those who come around to test the strength of your barriers. In other words, **if you** focus on boundaries, what you get is a whole lot of lessons in boundaries. No fun.

Instead, what's more **helpful** is to focus on what you want rather than what you don't. Focus on filling yourself up with your own energy, so there's no room in your field for anyone else. Essentially, this equates to self-love and self-trust, to feeling dark and light **and** whole and centered and balanced within, which expresses itself on the outside too. And then, without having to think about anyone else, only other balanced people come near. I have found that if I trust myself completely, then I don't have to **worry** about wondering who and what to trust in the outside world. If I were questioning who to trust, it would mean I'd likely attract energies and people I couldn't. On the other hand, if I'm vibrating at the frequency of trust, my intuition will only **lead** me to other trusting and trustworthy energies.

When we're relating **with** people in the physical world, boundaries are usually based on clear physical survival needs — like food, sleep, shelter, or relationships. We all have different needs, which change depending on the day. In subtle energy, it's the same, **only** we can't see them. But it's equally as important to know your own energetic space and your needs in relation to thoughts, beliefs, emotions, ideas, and patterns **in** order to upkeep a feeling of health and harmony there too. This can also change daily. And when we get to reading other people or things, this means it's important to always read yourself first.

Knowing what's going on in your own space also helps to know when you're picking up stuff that doesn't seem like yours. Then again, this one confuses me, because if like attracts like in energy, it means the places you find yourself in, the people you're surrounded by, the thoughts you notice others are choosing to believe, and of course, the people whose energy fields you end up being sensitive to *are* yours, in some regard. However, there is still always free will to choose how deeply to engage.

So let's say I'm feeling anxious one day, and because I'm vibrating at that frequency, my intuition might lead me to a similar frequency — for instance, to sit in traffic during LA rush hour. Well, in that case, I can't blame anyone but myself for the subconscious choice I made to surround myself with that type of energy. And hey, maybe I chose it because I knew deep down it was just the lesson I needed about how to work with anxiety! We could say the same for our interactions with people. For instance, maybe I was feeling anxious and called up a friend who was equally or even more anxious than I was. And it triggered me to let out a scream and release it. Well, in that case, knowing where my energy was before the call and allowing myself to have porous boundaries might've been exactly the thing I needed.

I know it sounds backward, but just consider it. In this way, you're taking responsibility for what resonates in your field. And in that, there's choice. And with choice comes personal power. Like the power to notice the anxious feeling, allow it to move through, and let it pass, like a big wave rolling up on shore and then retreating. And when I'm reading for someone who asks me to? I pay extra close attention to the messages that come through because they are often just as much for me as for them. These were taught to me as "matching pictures," which we'll get into in Section 2. But to wrap up here...boundaries. Yes, but also no. It helps to have them and also to let them flow. Set intentions for what you want based on your needs, and then let them go. The best boundary is simply to vibrate in a space of personal power and self-trust. So here's a good one for that...

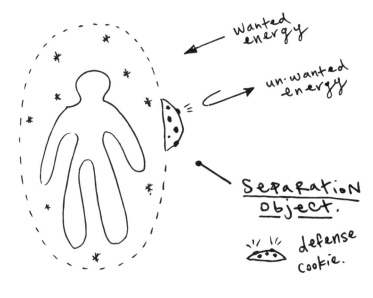

ENERGY TOOL #3:
Creating A Separation Object

This tool's been taught to me many different ways, but my favorite is this method that focuses on playfulness. Because of this, I've come to love this energy tool that makes me laugh every time I use it. That way, I'm focused on high vibes, silliness, fun, love, and trust. And so, when I use this, that's what ends up coming to me! Because with boundaries and separation, the point is not to wall ourselves off, but simply to make clear what we want (and don't want) to experience. This is helpful in daily life, and we'll use this when we get to reading others too.

To Open: Set an Intention

This is pretty much the best way to start any ritual or bit of self-energy work, or even any daily life task, really: Get clear on what you want to experience!

STEP 1: Plug in Your Energy

Use Energy Tool #1 to plug into Earth, Cosmic, and Neutral Grounding energy to align and balance, clear and reset your energy.

STEP 2: Call Back Your Energy

Use Energy Tool #2 for calling back your own energy, and feel it in your space.

STEP 3: Sense Your Energy Boundaries

A. Using your palms, see if you can sense where the edges of your aura or subtle body space are today. It may change depending on your mood or location. A typically comfy place is to have them around 1.5 to 2 feet away from your body, but this is up to you. With your aura cast out, you may sense a lot of what's around you; with your aura pulled in tight, you may feel contained or confined.

B. Practice pulling in your energetic boundaries — as in the edges of your subtle body or aura space — and pushing them out again, either using your palms or by visualizing doing this.

STEP 4: Create a Separation Object

A. Imagine a fun object at one spot in the edge of your field that can deflect energy. Mine is sometimes a ping-pong paddle or a harmonica that makes silly sounds as it travels around my field — again, it's up to you. You can use a scoop of ice cream that absorbs heavy beliefs into its chocolate chips or something. Have fun with it, watch it, play with it, test it out by setting the intention to keep out certain energies and invite other energies in, give it its own Grounding Cord, then...don't focus on it so much and just let it work for you.

To Close: Just Be

Forget about it and now just go about your day. Journal later on, or write about it here and see if you noticed any shifts!

write!

Hades & Persephone

Since we started this chapter with a Greek ghost, let's finish it with a good Greek myth before we get into the fun stuff of reading energy! Yin and yang doesn't just refer to darkness and light; it also refers to the formless and the formed, our internal vs. external lives, even intuition and logic and give and take and pretty much every other polarity you can think of. Over the course of our lives, we cycle through dark and light times, intuitive and not so intuitive periods, just like the weather cycles through cold and hot, rainy and dry. One of my teachers always says, when you're done clearing your plate, life always serves you more. Meaning some degree of darkness is pretty much inevitable, and it always serves to teach us something.

When I'm in these periods myself, the ancient Greek story of darkness and light, of Hades and Persephone, always perks me up to remind me of the bigger picture. And while I'm rushing it here, because, hey, you can Google this one — what happens is that the maiden Persephone is so purely made of light that she must marry Hades, lord of the Underworld, because she'd otherwise not know darkness at all. And so her father Zeus orchestrates the whole thing and she disappears down into deep depths of the Underworld. But do you know what happens once she's found and rescued by Hermes (ruler of communication, by the way) in order to come up to the light for six months of every year for all eternity afterward? The Earth comes into balance and Persephone herself evolves to become a queen. So, let's explore the depths, shall we?

Section 2: Working Your Voyance

ENERGY ReadiNg 101

6.

Now For The Fun Part :)

This is the section where we get to read energy! I mean, really we're all reading energy all the time — you're reading my energy right now as you read my words — but in this section, we're going to do it with more focused intention so we can see how great at it we already are. And it helps with understanding what source we're getting our energetic information from. How do you know if you're listening to your spirit guides or just the nagging voice of anxiety in your head? Or how do you know what's your "stuff" vs. someone else's? This is how. Why else is it helpful to learn to read energy in a conscious way? Well, it helps to develop intuition, and with it, a stronger sense of self-trust and inner knowing. Because when you realize you already knew, without having been told, say, that a total stranger on the other end of the phone is sitting on a mountain-top eating a bowl of oatmeal, well, not only does it feel really cool and magical, but it helps us trust our impressions. When you see how much you can know about someone else (when they're open to it, of course), how can you deny you know all the things about yourself too?

Just like doing math develops our aptitude for logic, practicing working with energy helps develop our intuitive skill. When you get a sense of how you read certain energies — for instance, one of my friends can smell a situation to do with relationships really well — or which signs you tend to pay attention to that inform your intuition — for instance, animals tell me lots about people in my life — it becomes much easier to receive tons of information, and you'll start to get more details too. With it, you can become much more familiar with your own inner workings, and you can become a wizard at working your own energy. Or you can just recognize that you already are.

Kelly & Her Meditation

Kelly is one of my favorite humans ever, and she calls herself one of the worst meditators around. She's super social, not one for private time, and because she doesn't love to just sit around and look within, well…it's never been her thing. Until one day when she found herself at a busy New York trade show, standing in front of a very caffeinated man in a pink neon shirt offering to hook her up to his new meditation machine.

To her, it sounded like the perfect time to take up this new hobby, and so she plopped herself down in his chair. "Ok, so, you sit here, all right?" he said, "and I'm going to hook up your iWatch to my screen, okay?" He grabbed her arm, "…and it's going to beep every time your mind wanders…" He poked her a bit, "…and it keeps score over here." He pointed to a giant screen with blinky numbers, grabbed her arm again, and started tinkering. She held back her laughter, turned her head away from the screen, and closed her eyes.

Of course, the machine started beeping right away. She tried not to open her eyes, but then she couldn't help it. She let her eyeballs follow some people passing by, heard beeping, then shut them again. She listened to a conversation about energy drinks, protein, and green foods as she heard the machine beep and beep some more. She burst out laughing, looked at the neon guy, and shrugged.

Later, she called to tell me the good news. "Court, I'm officially one of the worst meditators ever! Like 476 interruptions in five minutes!" She shared her story, way too proud of her accomplishment, giving me all the little details. And that's when I realized how focused she really is, because she could describe almost every single thing there. "Wow, Kell," I said. "You might suck at trade show booth meditation, but you're seriously one of the most tuned in people I know." And it's true. Only someone with that much presence can focus that intently. While she wasn't interested in tuning into her inner space, she was acutely aware of everything in the space around her.

So this is where I talk about the myth of being unable to meditate, ground, align, center, be present, of being dissociated, distracted, or out of tune. Because I don't buy any of it. And I know that personally, I can tune into twenty things at once or otherwise go very deeply into one. It can be in my external world, but likely because of who I am, it'll be in my internal one — it just depends on where my interest lies that day.

And I say this because one of our big blocks to meditating, feeling grounded, or centering ourselves is having decided that we're not good at any or all of those things. And I guarantee that when you're doing something you truly love, you can be present, grounded, and singularly focused, unless you're telling yourself that for some reason you can't.

Think of one of those things now — something you freaking love doing or even just love thinking about. Maybe it's snowboarding, making music, drawing, daydreaming about collecting lucky coins. Whatever it is, close your eyes for a moment and imagine yourself doing that thing. How does your body feel now? Centered? Present? In alignment? Meditative even? Good. Now that you're technically reading the energy of yourself when you're present, maybe even meditating, let's get into the many types of details you can pick up while you're in this state.

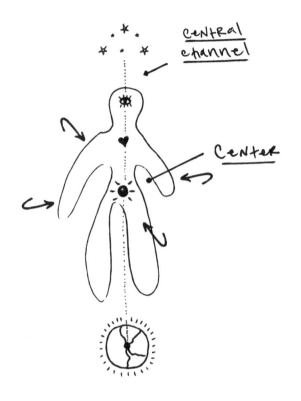

ENERGY TOOL #4:
Centering

Let's start with a proper exercise for centering. Why is it so important to get centered before we read? It's kind of like when you go fishing. To catch a fish, first you've got to reel in your line before you cast it out again with intention. Sure, you can fish with twenty lines out, but it will be a lot harder to reel in a fish if you've got a lot of them pulling at you. Reeling in your fishing line (or all of them) is kind of like centering. I try my best to walk around the world like this — my intuition never fails me when I do. Then, when you have an intention, a question, a direction you wish for your line to go, you can cast it out with more success. This also aligns third eye, heart, and gut!

You can do this with your eyes open, while you read off the page — or read through it first and then try it with eyes closed, which is easier for centering in your inner world. You can even record your own voice reading these instructions — whatever works! For best results, get your energy centered and then take some time to sit back and observe or walk around like this, so you get more comfy going about your day with your energy centered. Try this 12 minutes a day for seven days and see how it feels.

To Open: Feel Your Energy as It Is

Sit with your eyes closed and see how your energy feels right now.

STEP 1: Feel Your Core Central Channel

A. Pull your energy in and back by feeling your spine. If you're reading this on an object that's out in front of you, chances are your energy is partially out in front of you because of that. Typically, where the mind goes, energy flows. Feel the sensation in your body as you imagine drawing a line from the base of your spine all the way up to your crown.

B. Now draw a line down the front of your body, as if you had a spine there, from the crown to the base of the pelvis.

C. Next, imagine you have a spine running between the front and back of your body, feeling that center line — your body's **Core Central Channel**. Mentally trace that line from the base of the pelvis up to the crown center of your head. Do your best to feel into it.

STEP 2: Feel the Energy on Your Left Side

A. Now take a little walk around to the left side of your body. You can do this by feeling deeply into your left side, imagining you were standing just to the left of yourself, looking at your own profile. Check out the side of your face, your clothing, your body's posture, your feet on the ground from this position, and really feel the sensation of being slightly aligned left.

B. Release it, come back to center (because chances are it feels really awkward) and feel into your Core Central Channel.

STEP 3: Feel the Energy on Your Right Side

A. Now do the same thing on your right. This should feel pretty different from the left. Notice the sensations in your body as you stand on your right, again checking out the side of your face, your clothing, your body's posture, your feet on the ground from this position.

B. Release it, come back to center, and feel into your Core Central Channel.

STEP 4: Feel the Energy on Your Back Side ;)

A. Come to the back of your body, as if you could stand behind yourself and give yourself a little pat on the back. For most people, this feels difficult and a little weird — remember, it's only an exercise, so don't worry if this one is tough! Check out the back of your head, your clothing, your body's posture, your heels on the ground from this position.

B. Release it, come back to center, and feel into your Core Central Channel.

STEP 5: Feel the Energy out in Front of You

A. Last, circle to the front. This one should feel pretty familiar for most of us! But after coming center, it might not feel as good as it normally does — and that's the point! So let's not worry about spending too much time here: Check out your beautiful face, your clothing, your body's posture, and your toes on the ground, and then…

B. Come back to center again! Hold this position for a bit, taking a few deep breaths to relax into it.

To Close: Look out from Your Center

Try focusing your eyes on different places in the room to see if things look different when you're looking at them from your center. Speak them out loud, journal, or write about it here!

write!

_____

_____

_____

_____

...Now, go outside and go for a walk while feeling totally in your Center. Write about how that looks and feels, and what you notice!

write!

_____

_____

_____

_____

_____

_____

_____

_____

_____

_____

_____

Reading Energy

Now that you're centered and you know you can feel and sense your energy running in a few different ways, let's get into reading ourselves in a more focused way. Following are two classic reading tools: "Flower" and "Stick-Figure". While there are endless amounts of tools you can use to help develop your skill for energy reading and intuition, these are pretty popular. And they're pretty much the basis for being able to read anything! The flower technique is especially useful for sharpening your clairvoyance and developing a language of symbols, while the stick-figure will work your clairsentience and can help develop your skill for using a bunch of clair-senses at once! Try both and see which one works best for you.

If you're wanting to develop other senses, like clairaudience, or if you feel that other senses besides clairvoyance and clairsentience are already more developed for you, well, these tools will still open you up to getting more detailed messages in a bunch of new ways. Because by using them, you're sending a message to the energies like, *Hey, I'm ready for you to show up and speak to me now.* And on top of that, simply starting to read in a more focused way will open up and sharpen up your sensing abilities considerably. All you have to do is set the intention to do so! I recommend starting to read energy using your strongest sense, and then develop the others once you're comfortable using these tools.

And what if you're already super sensitive, reading energy all the time? These tools will give that energy a reliable place to show up, as opposed to, well, everywhere! That way, the cues and messages are just more helpful overall. The point is to give some structure to the formless energy we perceive, a recognizable form that feels familiar, that we can understand, like a bridge between the formed and formless worlds, so we can put to use in our formed world what the formless helps us understand. No matter who you are, your intuition will likely open up in a big way when you use these tools with intention. And if you're super sensitive, your connection (and comfort) with the formed world will open up too. At least mine did. So, I'm so happy to be able to share these. Enjoy!

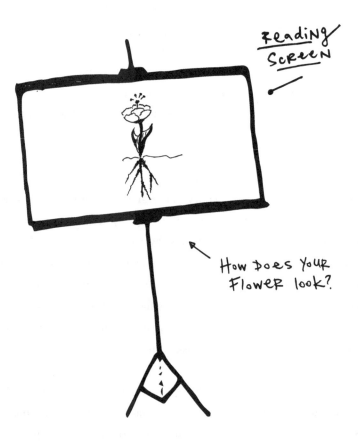

ENERGY TOOL #5:
Energy Reading, Flower Technique

So, first up is the flower tool. As I mentioned, this is such a good one for working your clairvoyance! A flower serves as a great metaphor for us humans; it's close enough that we can get helpful clues from it, but far enough that we're not reading too literally, so we can get used to reading in signs and symbols. Energy often speaks to us in metaphor, by giving hints and clues, underlying feeling tones. And this tool will help you develop your skill for *that*. Here's an example: Let's say you're feeling out of sorts. And so you read yourself and see that while your flower is very open to the sky, with a whole bunch of heavy open petals, it has no roots. It's about to fall over. Well, in that case, all you have to do is pull up some Earth Energy and connect your roots. If you do so as you're reading yourself, you will literally see your energy change before your very (third) eyes. ;) I recommend working with this one to develop your library of symbols, which we'll get more into in a bit. But first...

To Open: Set an Intention

Some good ones? To learn something new, be open to whatever comes, serve all beings everywhere for the greatest good, or even just to have fun and try something new. And by the way, I believe having fun is super high vibe and does serve all beings everywhere for the highest good, so you might check two boxes here.

STEP 1: Run Your Basic Energy Tools

A.   Start by Centering. (Tool #2)

B.   Release your Grounding Cord and create a new one to mark the present moment. Plug in and connect to Earth and Cosmic Energy. (Tool #1)

C.   Feel the boundaries of your subtle energy body, like a nice place to hang out in. We won't need to focus too much on our boundaries since we're only reading ourselves, but if you tend to pick up a lot of information on a daily basis, this is a good habit to get into. (Tool #3)

STEP 2: Create a Space for Energy Reading

A. Imagine a screen out in front of you, beyond the boundaries of your subtle energy body, and give the screen a Grounding Cord that is separate from your own. If you can't "see" it, just set the intention by pretending for now — both work.

B. Imagine a clear glass rose on the screen. (Side note: Classically this is taught as a rose, but I tend to see different flowers for different people right away. So you can start out with a rose and see what happens for you.)

STEP 3: Reading!

A. Now, imagine your own name written inside the rose or say your full name out loud, allowing your own essence to fill it. Sit back and watch, with your mind's eye, as the rose starts to develop some character.

B. Describe it out loud (because this helps to move energy through us): its leaves, petals, color, density, roots, crown, soil, the flowers surrounding it, how it's growing. Is it upright? Bent to one side? Wilted? Full of petals? Still? Moving? Tall? Short? What else do you notice yourself wanting to say about the rose?

C. Watch for a few minutes as the rose shifts form, as your camera lens shifts and shows you different angles, areas, and perspectives you may not have thought to look at.

To Close: Journal

Write or draw your results, like recording a dream, and see if even more details come! A flower or plant serves as a beautiful metaphor for us humans — close enough so we can understand, but far enough away that we can get a neutral reading.

*BONUS: Other Fun Things to Try!

- Read your energy in this way in the **morning** before work and then again at night when your day is done. Do **you notice** a difference?

- Read your energy after being solo for **awhile** vs. with a friend or other person. How does your flower look **different?** The same?

- Read your energy, then play a song that shifts your mood. How does the flower show up differently? The same?

...Record your results here!

write!

write!
_____
_____
_____
_____
_____
_____
_____
_____
_____
_____
_____
_____

ENERGY TOOL #6

YOU

YOUR stick figure

why one giant arm?

why one giant leg?

Observe... and ask questions about what you see, hear, feel, sense, taste!

ENERGY TOOL #6:
Energy Reading, Stick-Figure Technique

This is similar to Tool #5 for "Flower Reading," but you're going to use a clear glass stick figure instead of a flower. For some, it can be an easier way to access your skills for energy reading, especially for those who are more clairsentient. So, while you're doing this, pay close attention to the physical sensations in your body — maybe you can "see" and "feel" energy at the same time, or maybe even more of your senses will start to open up here. This one is really great for that!

To Open: Set an Intention

You know what to do! (Speak out loud what you'd like to experience.)

STEP 1: Run Your Basic Energy Tools

A. For fun, try them in reverse! Start by Centering. (Tool #2)

B. Release your Grounding Cord and create a new one, to mark the present moment. Plug in and connect to Earth and Cosmic Energy. (Tool #1)

C. Feel the boundaries of your subtle energy body, like a nice place to hang out in. We won't need to focus too much on our boundaries, since we're only reading ourselves, but if you tend to pick up a lot of information on a daily basis, this is a good habit to get into. (Tool #3)

STEP 2: Create a Space for Energy Reading

Imagine an empty glass stick figure out in front of you, beyond the boundaries of your subtle energy body, and give the figure a Grounding Cord that is separate from your own.

STEP 3: Energy Reading

A. Now, imagine your own name written inside the stick figure or say your full name out loud, allowing your own essence to fill it. Sit back and relax, allow the magic to unfold and watch, with your mind's eye, as the stick figure starts to animate in front of you or within you.

B. Describe out loud its posture and its position in the room. Is it floating? Grounded? Large? Small? Are there others around? Is there a color? Density? Texture? Is it even on both sides? How long are its legs and arms? Is it missing any legs and arms? Are there certain parts of the body showing up larger or brighter than others? Are you feeling numbness, density, bubbles, or tingling sensations in your own body?

C. Shift between looking at your visual avatar and feeling into your own body, working two clair-senses at once. What do you notice?

D. Watch for a few minutes — check out different perspectives, angles and areas you may not have thought to look at. Even try zooming in on a pinky fingernail!

To Close: Try Drawing It!

Try recording your results by drawing them and see if even more opens up. Everyone can draw a stick figure! Crayons are fun for recording rings or spots of color. And drawing from your intuitive space has the added bonus of opening up your intuitive channels even more! By using color, you might even enhance your ability to see colored auras or to intuit information in a whole new way!

*BONUS: Other Fun Things to Try!

• Read your energy and zoom in on your heart. What is it telling you?

• Read your energy like this and move from the physical body outward through the layers of your subtle body. What's different? The same?

• Read your energy, then get up and dance, shake, or do jumping jacks. How does the stick figure show up differently? The same?

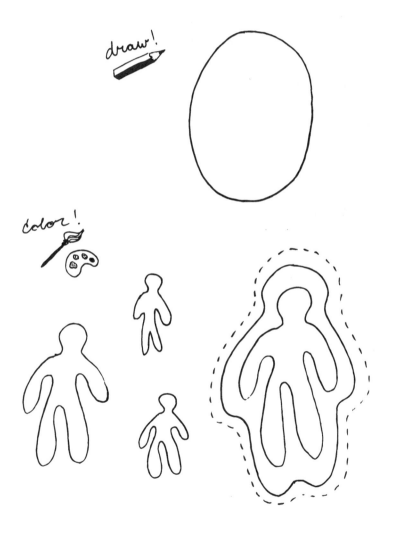

Tips For Best Results In Energy Reading

Here are a few things that make reading even easier:

1. **Say only what you see**: This keeps it as neutral as possible. For instance, if you see a bird flying into a pane of glass, simply describe that without trying too hard to interpret it. Understanding will come. This will be especially important for staying objective when you get into reading other people. As we already talked about, interpretation gets us in trouble if we're looking through a smudgy filter without realizing it. If we simply say what we see, we stay out of trouble, which is a good place to be. AND when we're reading ourselves, we get the added bonus of learning to accept whatever's happening. Goodbye self-judgment, hello more trust!

2. **Try not to fix anything**: While we're on the topic of acceptance, try simply observing without trying to fix whatever you see as a problem. When we acknowledge what's there, the energy usually balances out on its own. Or it invites more insight, or an intuitive hit comes through that helps reset completely. Energy is intelligent — it's pretty cool!

3. **Do less**: The easiest way to allow more energy to come through is to try less hard. By not trying to do much, we automatically go into a more receptive mode, which is the space of expert intuition! I like to think of making a wish on a dandelion and just blowing it away. Set an intention, then sit back and watch beauty unfold.

Eyes Open Vs. Closed

This might be pretty obvious, but I'm going to talk a little bit about why it's helpful to start to read with eyes closed. Because no matter how many times I teach this, I see that everyone wants to open their eyes the second they start reading. When reading for yourself, it may be obvious that you can "see" more of your own inner world with eyes closed. Yes, there are those who see auras with eyes open, maybe even half open or turned to the side, but there's more detail you can get when you truly focus on one thing: the formless world of energy. It seems weird to try to look at something with your eyes closed, but I promise it's a thing.

And when you're reading your surroundings for spirit guides and other beings? It helps not to be distracted by the objects we're used to focusing on in the formed world. We're shifting our perception here, and to try to "see" in a new way means looking in a new way too. What about reading others? Well, it is definitely easier to read with eyes closed (and even easier over the phone!) when we're not distracted or informed in some way by another's reaction to what we've said. Eventually, as you build up strength reading energy in your inner world, it will merge with the outer in a whole new way. And even if it already does? Creating different spaces for different experiences helps gain understanding, I've found. That being said, soon we're going to get into some eyes-open tools, so you can play with it all!

AAAND...Practice Of Course

Bonus point. By now, hopefully you're starting to see how learning to read intuitive cues consciously can be helpful. The yes and no answers we learned way back in Chapter 2 are insanely useful throughout the day, as is exploring deeper below the surface to get some details about what's really behind those decisions. And since you see how easy it is to read yourself when there's some intention behind it, imagine what other useful information is out there — er, in there — if we allow it to surface. Maybe you believe in guidance from the universe, or angels and spirits and guides, or maybe you're just curious how to better understand other people. In the next chapters, we're going to cover some useful tools for reading things like relationships, rooms, people, pets, and guides. Until then, practice. Getting good clear information about others and our surroundings starts with getting clear on ourselves. In energy reading, we are the antennae.

Your Energy Language Library

One of my teachers once said the reason we work with "essence" when it comes to energy — like sacred shapes, symbols, sound, scents, and color — is because it's universal. Just as binary code is a great language for organization, English is helpful for explaining ideas, and energy is most easily communicated through patterns and vibration — such as geometry, color, sound, texture, scent and more. When we're reading energy for ourselves, memories and "knowings" may come up, but as we're reading others and sharing what we "see," it helps to communicate in the language of energy, with signs and symbols. Deep down, we all have an understanding of it, even if we've temporarily forgotten. And since we have only some consensus on signs and symbols we're all familiar with, it's useful (and super fun!) to create your own library of signs and symbols.

My library came to me through noticing the signs and symbols in my life, and also practicing to read energy. When I'm reading for clients, I know if they want to talk about their current relationship because I'll see a glass box appear with another figure in it. If they're thinking about past relationships, I'll see many thought bubbles above them. A past relationship hangs out in the back of the figure I'm looking at, while something coming in the future will be in front. And so on. How and why did these become my symbols? I have no idea, but I'd seen them so many times in my readings that eventually, I knew exactly what they meant when they came up. In life, the symbols show up a bit differently for me, but I keep track of all of them so I can read the signs.

Exercise: Develop Your Energy Library

This is one of my favorites! Doing an exercise like this helps us understand even more deeply about how we get information — clairvoyantly, clairaudiently, clairsentiently, for example — while expanding our energetic vocabulary and our experience of perceiving energy. You might also notice you "see" images that have to do with relationships, while you might "feel" images that have to do with material things more strongly. It helps to pay attention and be open, keeping track of how each one shows up.

It's pretty much a word association game using our third eye vision. This is great to do with friends to get the quick impressions flowing, and to see how we really do all "see" so differently — or maybe to see how we share the exact same symbol with a friend! I once did this in one of my workshops, and two of my friends were sitting next to each other, but hadn't met before. They both saw a golden apple when I mentioned the word "teacher." That was really cool!

To do this, get a buddy and take turns having one person call out words while everyone else reads. Or, if you prefer to do it solo, record your own voice saying different words. To get focused and aligned, it helps to do this with eyes closed, pull your energy inward to Center, and plug into Earth, Cosmic, and Neutral Grounding Cord energy. Then, set the intention to let go of judgment and experience whatever comes. The reader will call out a word, wait 10 seconds to allow the readers to get impressions, and then everyone shares what they get. On the next page are a few word suggestions — but really, you can use anything!

I do this exercise in a lot of my workshops and it's always fun to see the range of symbols in the group. The picture I see for success usually has to do with a stick figure doing some sort of happy jump (yes, I see a lot of stick figures), but there are so many different responses. For instance, one woman in my group once reported seeing the color teal blue, while another saw their desk at work, someone heard the theme from Rocky, and yet another just felt expansive in his body like he was the sun. Another man saw a mountain climber and equipment, and interestingly, so did the woman next to him.

And there you have not just an example of each of our vastly different energy libraries, not just an example of how we all sense differently, but also the validation that these two people may have been using their abilities for telepathy without even realizing it. The more we talk about this stuff, the more we realize how good at it we already are. And the more we open up our library, the more intuitive cues can easily and effortlessly come through in our daily lives.

So, here are some words to get you started. It helps to keep a journal of what you see, hear, feel, taste, or smell so you have a guideline to refer back to, or you can write or draw here!

WORDS:

1. YES _____
2. NO _____
3. LOVE _____
4. SUCCESS _____
5. TRUST _____
6. SUPPORT _____
7. WORK _____
8. TRAVEL _____
9. STOP _____
10. GO _____
11. MOVE _____
12. STAY _____

Exercise: ***Validation***

This brings us to another important part of this whole thing: Validation. The more we're validated in using our sixth sense, the more we *know* we can rely on our abilities. Sharing with friends is great, and so is giving ourselves the validation we need. Write about times that your intuition was spot on. Then, keep these notes handy for the next time you question yourself. Because, hey, it happens! Think back…

Have you ever predicted that something was going to happen, even if jokingly or without much thought, only to later find out it did in fact happen?

_____
_____
_____
_____
_____

Have you ever been thinking about someone and then got a message from them a few seconds later? Or saw someone or something that reminded you of them?

_____
_____
_____
_____
_____

Have you ever been thinking something, and then got a text about it?

_____
_____
_____
_____
_____

Grandma V

Here's a fun story to get the juices flowing. I was reading in a group — group readings make for the best stories, really — and there were about five of us on the phone, each calling in from a different city. At that point in my life, I was still shy about mediumship and when I got my symbol for an ancestor wanting to come through — a head circling someone's head — I got a bit freaked out. So I was happy when I heard a loud noise coming from outside my house that meant I had to mute my phone and go investigate. I put my phone on speaker in my pocket, so I wouldn't break the connection we all had, and went looking for the source. It sounded like someone was banging on the door, only the noise was coming from the side of the house, as if someone were asking permission to come in through the wall.

Now, I live in an area with tons of squirrels and birds, and the animals can get loud sometimes, but I'd never heard anything like that before. I opened my door, stuck my head out the side window, banged on the wall from the inside, but couldn't see a thing. The noise got louder. Finally, without thinking much about it, I grabbed a handful of almonds and threw them out the door. A crow appeared above me then, perched on the skylight above my door, and started knocking frantically from...well, up above. Suddenly, I got it. I grabbed my phone, tuned back into my call only to hear another reader saying, "I'm getting you have a strong connection with a grandmother who's been trying to make herself known to you from up above." I burst out laughing, phone still on mute, trying to collect myself. I looked up and nodded to the beautiful bird. When the reader finished, I said, "Hey, this might sound like a weird question but...do you ever feed almonds to crows?" Our client went silent, but finally managed a, "yeeeah...why do you ask?" I told everyone the story of what had happened and our client burst out laughing. "Yup," she said. "Sounds like Grandma V — she was a very pushy lady." I looked up and noticed the crow had a big V-shaped bone in its mouth that must have been the reason for all the noise. The whole thing was astonishing, if not totally freaking cool and surreal. The reading finished with our client and grandmother rekindling a very strong connection, and it was another beautiful moment that shaped the way I understood reading energy from then on.

Energy Reading, Eyes Open

After this reading, I started playing with taking my reading out into my daily life. But it started in my private reading space with a practice we'll just call "Eyes Open Reading." Because I realized that as long as I'm in my reading space — that is, with my energy aligned and centered, having set an intention or asked a question — I can sit back, relax, and notice what I pay attention to and where my eyes go. It's like using your room as a Tarot deck, and it's very useful.

And yes, I know I just said a few pages back to read with eyes closed. And I'm still recommending that. In fact, I recommend practicing with all of these tools often, and even in combination. Why? Well, readings like this started to happen once I already had a lot of practice reading in the classic way. When I already had a well-developed energy library of signs and symbols, I was really familiar with the little sensations I get when reading, I could know when I was (and wasn't) in a good neutral reading space so I could get objective information. And it was easiest to develop that in a calm, focused, inward — in other words, eyes closed — space. In fact, you can start with an eyes-closed reading tool like the Flower or Stick-Figure and then switch to this one half-way through the reading to get a feel for it. When I work with clients, I still read in the classic eyes-closed ways I've shared with you (unless something big and bold like Grandma V's crow comes my way) because it really does help with staying focused inward.

In Chapter 10 we'll talk all about how to take this into daily life — noticing what we see, what gives us chills, a ping, or "the charge," as I like to call it, and allowing insight to unfold from there. For now, I'll say that, as with many of these tools, it's easier if you develop your skill for sensing on your own while reading yourself in a quiet, private and comfy-feeling space before you take it out in the world. That way, you know exactly what it feels like when you do!

ENERGY TOOL #7:
Reading Yourself, Eyes Open

With this one, you'll practice reading with eyes open, noticing what shows up in your space once you open a reading — kind of like what happened with Grandma V.

To Open: Set Intentional Prayers

Here's a good opening that I've learned from many teachers: Set an intention to read for the good of all beings everywhere and call in helpful angels and guides. I always ask Archangel Michael to be present to watch over a space during reading, Archangel Metatron to help me lovingly care for my sensitivity, Archangel Raphael for help with healing, and Archangel Gabriel for help with smooth communication. Help is always available, and it makes for a smoother, safer, more effective reading — so why not ask? We'll get into guidance and angels as we direct our reading focus outward.

STEP 1: Run Your Basic Tools

Figured I might as well mention this again.

STEP 2: Directing the Focus of Your Reading

Ask a question out loud. So simple.

STEP 3: Allowing Your Focus to Show You

Release expectation by simply feeling your body alignment, feeling heavy. Sit quiet and notice where your attention goes now.

What's the first thing you notice in the room? Seriously, pick the very first thing your attention goes to. Write it here:

_____

_____

What stands out about that object or spot in the room? Do you notice the sharp corners on a crystal vase, the shadows it makes or the way it lets light shine through? Or do you notice how small or large it seems next to everything surrounding it? Just allow your pen to flow — describe, rather than trying to interpret. Spend at least 4 minutes letting details unfold. Write it here:

_____

_____

_____

_____

List your body sensations and emotions as you're "reading." Spend at least 4 minutes letting details unfold. Write it here:

_____

_____

_____

_____

...Notice if your focus shifts to something else, if your body sensations change, and then write down your results like recording a dream. If it calls you, get out some drawing pens, pencils and crayons — sketching (especially with color!) can open your intuition up even more.

*BONUS: Other Fun Things to Try!

- Read your energy this way, setting the **intention** to find three objects that tell you something, like picking three Tarot **cards**. Do you get more detail?

- Read your energy like this after a **question** related to a relationship vs. life path stuff. What sort of patterns **are different**? The same?

- Read your energy, then clean and clear **your** space and do it again. How do the messages show up differently? The same?

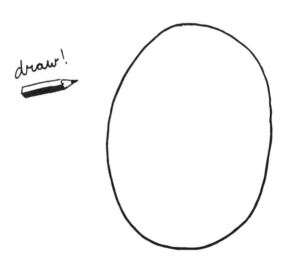

My First Reading

The first time I sat down to consciously do a reading, all I saw were blobs of color. I didn't know what I was looking for. I didn't know if I was making it up, or if I was seeing or feeling what I was supposed to be. For someone who was used to sensing so much, suddenly I questioned whether I could sense at all. Then again, there have always been times when I have questioned. And this was a big one. As I sat there doing the first exercise with my teacher, I could not manage the words to describe what only looked like a giant purple blob. I cried a little. It seemed silly. So nothing. So painful, and yet so healing to be doing this. And when someone related it to being blind and suddenly able to see, it put things in perspective and suddenly gave me my voice. Soon, I gave myself permission to say out loud what it is I saw, which made the blobs morph into shapes, then textures, then imagery, then sharp movie-like imagery, then sound and feelings and more.

After that, what used to pop into my head as unexpected (and sometimes unwelcome) knowings started showing up in this space instead — that is, in the space of conscious reading, during the times I'd actually asked or had been asked by someone to "see" and "feel" and "know." For someone who was once so disrupted by these unexpected unfamiliar "visions," it was a blessing. For someone who, like most of us, often needs guidance and reassurance that all's right for her in this world, it was nothing short of a miracle.

Reading Your Guides!

7.

The World Wide Web Of Trees

In *The Hidden Life of Trees*, author Peter Wohlleben writes about an underground web of fungus that runs beneath the forest floor. Scientists have observed that when roots choose to open their pores and be receptive, they make a connection to this great web that leads them to food. And then there are those trees who choose to go it alone, whose roots stay closed, and still manage to find food, but seem to work harder for it, zig-zagging around, changing direction more often than the ones who chose to connect to the web. Of course, who knows what's really going on? Maybe those are trees that just wanted to explore many options, like so many of us do, but here's where I'm going with this: If you were a tree or its roots, would you choose to connect to help if you knew it was available? Right. So, let's talk energetic guidance. We've all heard before that the Universe has our back, that we have help, that we are guided along the way, but what happens when you desperately want to believe that but have no clue if it's actually happening or where to start looking? Or what if you're not sure if you should be listening to the voice that sounds like it's trying to guide you but is instead leading you to do uncomfortable things? What if you've felt so super connected at times, but now it seems you've lost contact with your source of guidance? Or the message are kind of fuzzy? How do you reset and re-connect?

Spirit Guides & Guidance

As you've probably noticed by now, there are many different types of energy you can connect to. Some are more helpful than others, and at different times. Here, I'm going to focus on what's always reliable, both in daily life and for when you want to do a focused energy reading. The sources I connect with primarily are guides, angels, ancestors, and other patterns of energy that serve to teach me about my highest potential, like deities and mentors. There are even forces of nature that I look to for wisdom. Sacred geometry and crystals can also represent a higher intelligence — for instance, have you had the experience of being in the presence of something so simple-seeming as a clear quartz crystal, a clean room, a pristine spot in nature, and experienced a new type of insight or clarity within?

So how do you know if you're consulting the best source for guidance? The best way to start, or to re-establish a connection after some time away, is to develop the connection while you're in a quiet, inward-looking space without distraction, focused on your own highest good rather than on someone or something else. From there, you can get familiar with all the sensations associated with receiving that juicy higher guidance, and then you can take it out into the world.

But what if you're out in the world and unsure about your source of guidance? Well, if I'm trying to get higher guidance but notice I'm also craving something that isn't good for me, for example — like a piece of cheese that's going to give me a tummy ache later on — I know I'm not currently acting according to my highest good. In other words, if I'm in a space of harming myself rather than helping myself, even if only slightly, I know I have to take a second to reconnect with my intentions, my highest angels, guides, and vibes, before I do anything else. Of course, if I still want that cheese, I'm probably going to go ahead and eat it (and love it) anyway and enjoy the bed rest I take as a result of it afterward too. We're complex creatures, of course, but this is such an easy way to gauge.

I get clients on the rare occasion asking me about a voice they think is their guide directing them to do harmful things. To which I say: That is probably most certainly not your guide. Use the tools provided in...well, all of this book and beyond, especially chapters 4 and 5 on darkness and clearing filters...to make sure you're nurturing your body, mind, and spirit, loving and accepting all your parts. A good therapist or holistic health practitioner can be a great resource too. And even if you're not making perfect choices all the time — hey, none of us are perfect — the way you feel when you're working toward helping yourself will connect you to a source of guidance that assists in a happy, healthy, balanced human experience.

And like I've said, while there's nothing to fear, it helps to know what you do and don't want to spend time with. As with people, places, and spaces, you always have a choice about what to connect to. It's simply about where you choose to focus. And just like you choose the friends you hang out with, you probably want to be choosy when it comes to the formless world too. Since we're in the driver's seat of our own bodies, steering this thing like a car, we are completely in charge.

I do get questions about how different types of guidance show up. It's different for everyone, but here's my best attempt at a description: My higher guidance system feels smooth, flowing, like home. My destructive guidance system feels more like a pull, a scream, an anxious decision made from a place of weakness, lack, wanting, pain, even addiction. The two look and feel very different. I might see soft violet waves or feel instantly peaceful and calm when I meet with an energy that's serving me. When I've met with one that's helped me destroy a piece of myself instead (which has sometimes been necessary), it's felt like a rope has lassoed itself around my waist and pulled me toward a person, thing, or situation, after which I've seen, in an instant, a blur, a mess, or the color red.

And while receiving guidance doesn't always mean life is going to be perfect — because sometimes we do need the lessons that help to clear our more difficult patterns — it's helpful to know what you're working with, so you're able to choose. So with that, here's an energy tool that builds on what we've been working with to strengthen the connection with higher guides.

ENERGY tool #8

← Guide!

← Guide OR Maybe an ancestor — ASK!

... It's Really this Easy. AND worth it! ☺

ENERGY TOOL #8:
Reading Your Guides

So, reading guides is easy. We'll build on Tool #6 for "Stick-Figure Reading" and rather than focus the lens on our own energy body, we're going to zoom in on what's around it instead. To help connect to a neutral Earthly source (because we want help here on Earth, right?), it's extra important to start off by plugging in your energy. I always call upon Archangels before doing this exercise, so I'm working with high vibrations, and I suggest you do the same.

To establish connection, simply focus on what your guides "look" and "feel" like for now — how you perceive them — rather than ask a specific question. That way, you know you're not being biased in any way and can simply feel the pure presence of your team of guides.

To Open: Focus on the Quality of Energy You Want to Connect With

How do you want your life to feel? Guided, helped and easy breezy, right? So first things first, think of a time in your life when you felt exactly as you want to feel now — for instance, highly guided and so super happy. Close your eyes, put your hand over your heart, and bring up a memory of a time when you felt that way, even if it was brief and long ago: What did the air smell like at that moment? How did it feel across your skin? How did your body feel? What was your facial expression? An emotion you felt? Who or what was surrounding you? Is there a song that describes this moment? Feel into your heart space now.

STEP 1: Run Your Basic Energy Tools

Release your old Grounding Cord and create a new one, to signify that you're in a new moment. Plug in to Earth and Cosmic Energy. Center and feel your Core Channel, your Separation Object. Feel your own auric space.

Optional: Light a candle, sit in a special spot (perhaps in front of your altar or on a pretty pillow), find a special object, or dab on your favorite essential oil...so there is a special setting, scent, or object you can use to evoke this energy time and again.

STEP 2: Announce That You'd Like to Connect With Your Guides

With your hand still on your heart, still in that lovey high vibe space, announce out loud that you'd like to connect to your guides. And you can even add a statement about why, since some of us have different guides for different purposes:

- Do you want to connect to guidance for help with partnership and starting a family?

- To get insight about your path and purpose?

- Because you're just curious for now to know more about your guides, what they look like, feel like, even taste like, a name you can call them by, a sign they can give you when they're in your midst?

...Take a moment to get clear on this and then speak it out loud.

STEP 3: Create a Space for Energy Reading

Imagine an empty glass stick figure out in front of you, beyond the boundaries of your subtle energy body, and give the figure a Grounding Cord that is separate from your own.

STEP 4: Energy Reading!

A. Now, with eyes closed, imagine your own name written inside the stick figure or say your full name out loud, allowing your essence to fill it.

Then, focus your inner gaze on the area around the figure. This time, we're going to watch the area OUTSIDE the stick figure body. Sense any colors, characters, blobs of energy or even sounds near the figure out in front of you. You may even feel or hear something around your physical body!

B. Describe the details out loud: its position near your body — for instance, above your head or off to one side or the other. Are there colors, sounds, even characters you're familiar with that come to mind? For instance, one person's guide could be like Wonder Woman while another "looks" more like an old Buddhist monk or a figure that's more like an essence and not recognizable at all. And how many are there? Are you feeling warm spots, bubbles, or tingling sensations in your own body? Are you having memories or images come up of ways they've tried to communicate with you (e.g., you found feathers or coins, or you saw a special animal or tracks in the sand)?

C. Shift between looking at your visual avatar and feeling into your own body, working two clair-senses at once. What else do you notice? If you don't sense much, feel into the areas surrounding your subtle body, about three feet away from you.

To Close: Ask for a Sign!

Write about what you "saw" or "felt" like recording a dream. To open up even more, draw (with color!): Where do your guides like to hang out? What do they look like? Color? Texture? Theme? What does the overall vibe of each guide tell you about your long-term goals here on Earth, or your purpose? For instance, if I had a Wonder Woman guide, it might tell me I'm here to be a hero for women, and so forth...you know what to do.

When you're done, ask each guide to show you the best way to connect with them in daily life — for instance, through songs, coins, an animal crossing your path. And make sure to thank them always — every being loves to be appreciated for their service, even guides!

*BONUS: Other Fun Things to Try!

- Read your energy this way and ask a specific question: How does the information come through? Is it different than when you were reading yourself?

- Write a letter to your guides first, then read your energy like this, and ask for words to come through: How do they show up? For instance, do you hear a sentence, a song, or see a typed message in your mind's eye? What happens if you grab a pen and let it float across the page? Allow words to flow out your mouth?

- Read your energy, sitting in meditation for a good 5 minutes. Do you get more detailed information? Or do you get more when you're writing, drawing, speaking out loud, or simply noticing signs?

...Write about your guides here! (And thank them here too!)

write!

_____
_____
_____
_____
_____

...Draw about your guides here!

Angels, Ancestors, Guides & "Dark" Energies

Let's talk angels, spirit guides, ancestors, and other beings you might connect with. Truthfully, there's so much out there, probably a lot more than this tiny psychic can comprehend, and to go over all of it is for another book. If you want to nerd out on this topic, Doreen Virtue and Sonia Choquette's books and audibles are some of my favorites. Mostly, they like to keep it high vibe and so do I, even though I believe everything has its place and I honor the full spectrum in our world of polarity and beyond. But when I call on help, I know I, for one, would rather ask a source I truly want to get guidance from. Like if you ask your crazy Uncle Bernie who was terrible with money about how to make your first million, you might be seriously disappointed with the results. But if you ask your friend who's always smiling for some tips on happiness, well, then you're more likely to get what you're looking for. It helps to get clear on what sort of energy you want to experience and go from there. It's my belief that we all have access to our own personal source of higher guidance within, as well as a support team available to us at all times. So here's a bit more on that.

Angels

As you know by now, wherever your focus goes, energy flows, so if you focus on having a good time, you end up investing your energy in high vibes and you'll end up attracting high vibe patterns of energy — like angels! When I feel or "see" angels in my vicinity, I feel giddy, bubbly, peaceful, relaxed, and blissed. Imaginative, creative, and playful. Unconditionally supported, safe and in my flow. I see sparkles, pretty pastel colors, and brightness. I hear tingly sounds and bells. I experience synchronicity after synchronicity, which I like to call little miracles, and depending on how they show up, I associate them with different angels.

All you have to do to connect with the energy of angels is call upon them, be open to receive their gifts and presence, and they come near. Because they exist in energy form, they are not bound to time and space and can visit us all at the same time if we so choose it. In other words, if we call on angelic energy, it's not like we're hogging it or taking it away from anyone else, so you might as well call upon them often. It feels good and supportive to ask for their help. I call on angelic support for every reading I do, and I suggest you do too, for best results. Because if help is available, why not ask?

In my readings, I ask for help from Archangel Michael for a safe space, Archangel Gabriel to help with clear communication, Archangel Raphael for help with healing, and Archangel Metatron for help clearing energy. Certain cultures have other names for referring to angelic energies, but since I grew up in the Judeo-Christian sphere, these ones speak to me. And there are many more Archangels and deities you can work with — check my website for resources. I urge you to use the tools above to go into your meditative space with the intention of reading angelic energy and see what comes up! Perhaps they'll even show you how they've been communicating with you all along!

Guides

Now I'm fully aware that some of you may not believe in angels or guides or ancestors helping us along our way, and that's fine. We all have a different relationship with this, and ultimately, it doesn't matter what you like to use as your compass — perhaps it's simply your older, wiser self, which works great. I urge you to use ideas you feel most comfortable with, for best results. That being said, I've seen that everyone I've ever read has some sort of inner GPS guidance system, or at least one character (usually more) hanging around them that I like to refer to as a Guide.

In comparison to angels, I find that my guides feel more like a system offering direction. They're a little more serious, trying to steer me this way or that, and they ultimately feel reassuring. They seem to want me to get down to business, to focus on and complete my lessons, even if it's simply about being in the flow and having fun sometimes. So, rather than bubble sparkles, they feel more like talking to an old wise friend, stable and comforting, always with a specific message to give. In my reading space, they usually appear as a shape or character that represents the lesson or mission they're here to help with, whatever we're talking about. Like

I might see one dressed as Wonder Woman (you can tell I love her) if a female client's tasked with stepping into her feminine power. I've seen healing guides that looked like masters of a specific tradition, other superheroes, elders, even ancestors. I am intrigued by, and in awe of guides. And I'm pretty sure it helps to be in reverence of this system tasked with helping us — even if we're really just giving love to our inner selves — because, hey, doing this Earth thing is sometimes an exhausting job. I try as often as possible to thank my guides for all they're teaching me, for all they've given me, and to acknowledge I can hear them when they give me a message.

Certain signs, symbols, and synchronicities will tell me of lessons from my guides — for instance, certain number sequences will tell me if something has to do with my work, with helping a person, with simply relaxing and having fun. Sometimes the messages are more jarring, clear, like a parent — as in my phone suddenly dying even though my battery's at 70% when I'm having a conversation that isn't serving me or when I'm about to text someone I probably shouldn't. It just feels so good to cultivate a relationship and method of communication with inner guidance. To do so, simply sit in your meditative reading space often, as illustrated above, and ask for messages and signs from your guides, maybe even memories from the past that help with communication — for instance, memories of certain people tell me about lessons I'm revisiting. Always be clear on how you'd like to receive messages from guides in daily life — they will always show up, so long as we just sit back and allow them to come through! And whether you listen to the advice or not, remember to always give thanks for the communication.

Ancestors

I believe we are born into certain families or soul groups that help us complete the spiritual tasks and lessons we're given on this Earth — people who can teach us about the challenges or difficult ideas and situations we're meant to overcome. It can be anything from getting over fear of financial insecurity to uplifting generations of cultural oppression, sexual repression, or even becoming open to having more fun. You likely know deep down about the recurring themes in your life. Many of them are generational and societal, and you probably share certain themes with others you find yourself **hanging** around, beyond the people in your family and ancestral line.

When someone is working through the heavy beliefs or boundaries imposed by previous generations, I tend to see their ancestors hanging around closely. Some of my teachers have said we can announce to our ancestors that we're done dealing with their lessons, but to be honest, I haven't had luck with this. I'm not sure if that's because I came here to do this work specifically or because I have an unconscious need to heal, so you may want to try this out for yourself and see. In any case, it has been shown that we carry our ancestral patterning and therefore its energy in our bone marrow, so our DNA is producing cells imprinted with this stuff. However, there are scientists who provide good evidence for the fact that we can change it. Bruce Lipton's book *The Biology of Belief* gives a great argument for why we're not stuck with ancestral patterns. I've also done some great Yoga and Qigong practices that are designed to help clear ancestral trauma.

When you receive guidance from ancestors in spirit, you can choose to take the advice or leave it be. As I've said before and will say again, would you want to ask your wild Aunt Jannie who was single her whole life for advice on marriage? Maybe, maybe not. But would you ask her to stand by you in the kitchen if she was a great cook? Probably a better bet. When I'm reading — and living, actually — I simply ask my ancestors in spirit to stand behind me in loving support until I want to come to them with an actual question, just as I would've done when they were alive. That being said, the line gets blurred sometimes and I am sooo grateful for all the wisdom and gifts and resiliency that has come before me through my ancestors, so much so that sometimes I hold up my hands just to feel the warm touch of my grandmas in spirit.

To connect with yours, you can use the energy tool above and ask instead for your ancestors to appear, ask how you can know they're there. For some, it comes easier in dreams. I feel my grandmothers cooking with me, crafting with me, adventuring with me, even writing this with me, and I know I can call upon them to feel loved at all times. If you're having trouble connecting, sit quietly and think of pleasant times you shared, and then wait and see what comes up.

"Dark" Energies

Now I'd love to gloss over the less savory-feeling energies, of our ancestors or our surroundings, but I don't think it's useful or fair. We've already discussed the importance of yin and yang, dark and light, experiencing all this great Earth has to offer. And just like there is anger and sadness in this world, there are energies associated with mischief, misfortune, and pain. I see "dark" energies as heavy, disempowering belief systems — for instance, the belief that all men or women are this or that. If we're tuned to a certain belief system (or energy), we attract more of it. That's why it's important to pay attention to your intentions, words, thoughts, actions and beliefs — ultimately you have the power to choose what sort of energy you attract and therefore experience.

Some high vibe spiritual teachers will tell you they don't believe in exorcisms from heavy energies. But let me tell you, I have had a few. Mine came in the form of experiencing grief and physical pain, even skin rashes and hives, due to releasing once held heavy beliefs (AKA "dark" energies) such as "No one will want to read this book because no one cares what women have to say." Is that true? No way. Does this seem big and dark and scary? For me, it did. Now it sounds silly in hindsight, but when I saw the energy of it come up, and out, it was mentally, emotionally, and physically painful. The energy of that one in particular seemed to fly out of my body, making the sound of a hurt dog. And it scared me, but only for the few minutes before I realized I was free. Afterward, I felt 10 pounds lighter. And best of all, I knew that because I could see (and hear) it floating away, it was no longer holding me back from speaking or writing. In my case, what started out as a dark and fearsome energy gave birth to something beautiful — this book.

But I'll say it again: For maximum comfort and ease, choose wisely who and what you connect to for guidance. If "dark" stuff feels like it's overpowering you, refer back to Chapter 5 for working with shadows or visit a good therapist or holistic health specialist. While we're at it, here's a useful little ex-orcise to help you move onto higher vibes when it feels like you're stuck in the lows. Ultimately, getting in contact with the dark shadowy stuff is a great opportunity for transformation, so long as you're not addicted to suffering or defining yourself by it.

<u>Ex-orcise</u>: Transforming "Dark" Energy

This doesn't have to be gory like you see in movies, but if it does get to be dramatic...well that's up to you. For this one, grab a pen and paper, and maybe even text your favorite witchy best friend, so you have a reminder that you are loved and supported, even in the dark times. And if not, here's my nugget of love and support to you: Remember, what's another "dark" energy? The belief that life is scary or hard or punishing — it doesn't have to be. Write a letter to your heavy energy, in all its messy, struggling, victim-sounding glory. It can go something like...

Dear Ghost / Entity / Lord of the Dark Force of My Shoe Closet / Self Who Always Chooses to Sabotage Me When it Comes to _____ ,

I'm breaking up with you. I'll admit that I've been scared of cutting ties with you for some time now. The way you make me _____ (ex: miss my Uber even though I called the driver 20 times / always late on deadlines / texting back women or men I shouldn't even be dating) has me feeling_____(ex: powerless) and_____ (ex: like no one ever helps me / like I'm bad at work / like I'm never going to meet someone I like). And I'm ready to be over and done with this mess. Because I know that my time is worthwhile, my sheer presence and energy is a gift, and I don't want to waste it by_____(ex: arguing with a stranger over cancellation fees / over-explaining / spending too much time on my phone). And while we're on the topic, I don't want to have to_____(ex: worry about money anymore either / care about what people think of me / stress about finding love). And_____(this is the part where you just freely rant, just get all the juice out) and_____ (might as well go for it even more). So, I hereby release the need to feel_____(ex: sad, mad, guilty, ashamed, frustrated, like a total loser, victim) and at odds with myself, because I recognize it's no longer serving me. I now declare that I'm beautiful and powerful and lovable and supported and _____ and I know I create my own destiny. I am so EXCITED and free and done with this s*^t and_____!!!! Amen.

Now, read your letter out loud — speaking moves the energy and makes big shifts happen even quicker — and cry and scream if you feel like it, because that moves energy too. Pillows and cars and deserted spots in nature are good scream spots because they won't scare the neighbors. Your energy is best dealt with by you alone, maybe with a friend or healer standing by for support, then given to the Earth for transformation, not given to someone else so they have to deal with it too. After you've felt your feelings, cross out your letter, tear it up, or even burn it up and feel the "dark" energy as it is released and transformed, to be made into something new, shiny, and beautiful. Like wisdom and insight. Lightness and more room for newness and joy. And while we're at it, why not do a little celebration dancing-like-a-maniac sort of thing? Or some shaking? When you work with energy, you always want to release your thoughts, emotions, *and* your physical body for best results. Doing this in nature, by an ocean or body of water, or following it up with a cleansing salt bath or shower and tons of water to drink is helpful — filling yourself up with love and nourishment after the clearing.

Raising Your Vibes

In order to raise your vibration, you only need to focus your mind on a time when your vibe was high — such as thinking of a synchronicity, a beautiful coincidence, a "little miracle," as I like to call them. Following is one of mine. After you read it, I encourage you to remember one of your own. If you can't think of one (yet!), close your eyes after you read mine and write about all the sensations you feel afterward. And if it makes you want to barf, feel angry, sick, or annoyed, then great. Write about *that*, then give yourself a little ex-orcise, clearing whatever has been blocking you up to this point from receiving solid high-vibe guidance.

Ocean In View, O The Joy!

One Sunday, I woke up with a long list of stuff to do, with no love for any of it. I got in the shower, caught a glimpse of myself in the mirror and almost fell down. My face was long and sour-looking, as I thought of all the stuff I should be doing but wasn't. I got the urge to go to the beach. It was raining, but I decided I didn't care. I got in my car and drove toward the coast. When I got close, the sun started to peek out, and as I pulled in to park, the rain stopped altogether. Since it wasn't really beach weather, I walked out to shore with no other person in sight. It was just me, the ocean, the cliffs, and cypress trees. I huddled in my blanket, feeling totally blessed, giggling to myself as I sat there gifted with what felt like such a rare opportunity. I pulled out my journal to write, *maybe all we need in life is to set aside our to-do lists and just be in joy.*

When I was done, a black bird hopped up to me. He got close and I sat trying not to move so I wouldn't scare him. He bounced straight up to my knee, looked me in the eyes, peeped for a second, then hopped over to a few feet in front of me and pointed his beak at a coin in the sand. He waited while I grabbed for the coin and studied it: On it was ocean, cliffs, and cypress trees. I could hardly believe it! It looked just like my pretty little scene. And on it said, "Ocean in view, O the joy." I laughed so hard, I cried. Then my little friend showed me the bright neon orange beneath his wings and flew off.

Now, for those who know and work with angels, you could say this is the trademark of Archangel Gabriel, who's said to communicate through the written word, but who really knows for sure? I do like to think Gabriel is with me, nudging me along in creative pursuits and reminding me at every turn to find joy and humor in things, to always speak my truth. But hey, even if you want to pass this off as an awesome coincidence, you've got to admit it's cool.

...Do you have a story of synchronicity? Write about it! Raise your vibe!

How To Get Daily Messages From Your Guides

When you open yourself up to receiving guidance via intuition, it is always available. And yes, I've found that sometimes answers can be tough and not exactly what I've wanted to hear, but by establishing a connection simply by "looking" at my guides or "feeling" them in my reading space, I know I'm guaranteed at least one easy and neutral way to establish a connection. Because when you do that, you're not asking for guidance on anything in particular, other than for how to connect with your angels and guides! So what are some other ways you can connect to guidance?

1. **Name them!** You can name your guides and remember where they seem to hang out around your body — you can even look toward them if it helps you connect.

2. **Notice how guidance shows up**: Know how each one tends to give you guidance and on which topics — is it mostly through objects? Coins? Songs? Memories? Even through a mistyped text or messages from friends?

3. **Pay attention to the details**: Remember the signs and symbols that come through and notice when, where, and how you asked. Was it a specific time of day? In nature? In an elevator? While doing dishes? After asking out loud? In your journal? As a text to a specific friend?

...And if you already have a well-developed repertoire, go ahead and expand it a little! Keep track of your guided messages and your results in a journal, keep objects that have helped guide you on an altar, as a token of appreciation, as a reminder for those times when you might forget how guided you really are.

Calling In Guides For Reading Energy

So it seems obvious why it's helpful to have a support team of guides, angels, and ancestors present in daily life, but why are they so helpful to invite into your reading space? I think it's similar to asking an elder to give you advice about life. Sure, they may have walked a different path than you, they may have different and sometimes weird opinions, but they've ultimately got some stuff to share about this earthly plane, simply by virtue of having been here awhile. They know tons about things like...say, why you never let a shopping cart roll into your car at full speed. Things we otherwise might not think of. I figure inviting high vibe guides and angels to a reading is sort of like asking for help navigating the spirit plane, in much the same way. And it's an important step I was taught by every single one of my teachers, mentors, and elders in these practices. I have honestly never met a mentor or teacher who didn't have a strong connection with their team of spiritual guides. To connect more deeply, we must spend time with our guides and get familiar with their presence and their wisdom, which — much like visiting with a really cool grandma — warms your heart and gives a sense of security and assuredness only an experience like that can bring.

So for best results (in life, really), establish a good strong connection to your spirit team. And how do you do that? Simply by communicating with your guides often! Soon we're going to start reading others, and for that, you're definitely going to want to call in the help of angels and guides, so go ahead and ask them a question or send them a bit of thanks right now!

Reading Others

8.

Reading Other People

Oooh, so now comes the good stuff. If you've ever had any sort of psychic, intuitive, or energetic reading, or even a healing conversation with someone who just seemed to know, you're probably pretty curious about how this works. My friend Ethan called me the week I was editing this chapter (of course) and said, "Hey, I just had a conversation with a psychic who spoke word for word a private conversation I had...like how, Courtney...how?!" He was confused, if not a little freaked out. The truth is that anyone can do it. I've said it before and I'll say it again: We're all reading each other all the time. But just like all of us can pick up a pencil and make some sort of drawing, yet some of us are able to draw with so much detail that our sketches look like photos...well, it's kind of like that. Obviously Ethan was thinking a lot about this conversation, so much so that it was in his field, and like a highly tuned radio antenna, the woman who read him honed in on the details. Just so none of us are walking around scared that our bank info's going to get stolen by psychics, I will say this is rare. I like to think of sensitivity like a bell curve. We can all sense into things, but only a few can do it with that much accuracy.

So I suppose the next question is, How is this useful? Well, from a healing perspective, it's good to know what's floating around in your field so you can choose if you want to hold onto what's there — such as Ethan's conversation, which was definitely not something he wanted to repeat. Our experiences create imprints that other humans we relate with can pick up and respond to. So let's say Ethan's convo with this person was a bullying one; it would be kind of like he was walking around with a "kick me" sign in his field that everyone could energetically read, and then they'd kick him accordingly. But if Ethan suddenly became aware of the imprint — this "kick me" sign, so to speak — he could make a choice about whether or not he wanted to keep wearing it. In other words, he could make a decision to clear that filter from his field. Isn't that cool? So, you can use these practices to, like, just improve your life. No biggie.

Another reason this stuff is useful? Well, if you're not 100% confident in your ability to read your own energy, but you turn out to be awesome at reading someone else's, then you kind of have no choice but to change your mind about yourself — that is, you can trust yourself better. And that just makes life a whole lot easier. I mean, how many times have you gone on a roller coaster with someone, only to say later, "I knew they'd be trouble the second I met them." It's with our sixth sense we get that split second of knowing, and then our five senses kick in and jumble it all up, adding an extra layer of fun. Or maybe not so fun, especially when we knew better.

But isn't it a major boundary cross, and sometimes uncomfy and unnecessary to read others, you might ask? Yes. In daily life, it often is. But, when you start reading others in a conscious meditative space, and for the sake of learning, your intuitive abilities can increase tenfold. Why? Because in it, we receive validation for how psychic we are. If there's one way to know for sure that you are super freaking intuitive, it's to practice using your intuition and have it confirmed by someone you know and trust.

And what if that someone-you-trust isn't you yet? When I began consciously reading my own energy, I wasn't sure I could trust what I was getting. When I began consciously reading my surroundings, I wasn't sure I could trust what I was getting. In relationships with ancestors, guides, and other spirits, I wasn't sure I could trust what I was getting...but when I began reading totally accurate details of a random stranger's breakup? Well when that happens, it's pretty mind-blowingly hard not to trust what you're getting. An added bonus? You pretty much always learn a little something about yourself in the process because like attracts like in energy. That is, when we use our five senses, we look for differences between two things — like one shade of pink versus another tells us what color we're looking at — but when we read energy and use our sixth sense, we look for what's the same. Like your new-in-this-city energy kinda feels like mine. And really, we can only recognize the energetic pattern of something we've experienced. Because of this, reading others breeds compassion and self-compassion. So in this chapter, we get to the goods. Here is where we can really experience, in a conscious way, what it is to have an energetic connection with others.

On Ethics

But first, a little PSA on ethics. Just like you want to be invited over to someone's house, rather than breaking in, you want to get permission to read someone. First off, if you sneak into another person's energy field, they will know something's up and they probably won't like it. So be prepared for that. Remember, we are ALL super freaking great at sensing energy. So I repeat: Even if you haven't told someone you're reading their energy, they will know and their behavior around you may change.

When you read energy, you're also moving energy — like if you snuck into someone's house, you might leave footprints or move a painting. And when you're in any sort of relationship, this movement of energy will also affect the way someone perceives you and will bring up issues of safety and security. So if you go snooping, just for the sake of it, it could backfire. For instance, it may cause someone to build up their boundaries or wonder if you're someone they can trust. Which makes sense, because if you're reading someone's energy rather than asking them a direct question, you're energetically sending the message you don't trust them to answer honestly, nor trust yourself enough to ask. In fact, I've found that when I accidentally start to read someone, my intuition is often telling me there are issues related to trust between me and that person.

Because of all this, I don't share impressions I get about other people unless they ask me or unless it feels important, in which case I ask first if they'd like me to share. This is something I've learned the hard way — by virtue of having accidentally shared too much info way too many times. Also, I've been taught by many great mentors to always mind my own business, reel my focus back when this happens, and so I do. And it's been wonderful. Personally, I find the most helpful part about picking up random bits of information tells me when I'm out of alignment with myself, afraid or un-trusting, and serves as a signal for me to look deeper within my own energy field. Unless there's actual danger of course, in which case, I get out of the way and thank my sensitivity and my guides.

When we're talking reading relationships — as in a client's asked for help with their relationship — I am reading my client's energy as opposed to the person they're in relationship with. Why? Because my client's field is telling me about the type of relationship they're in, the dynamic they're having trouble with. Their relationship with the other person simply reflects their "stuff" back. A confusing concept, I know, but just stick with me on this one until you "see" it for yourself when we get to reading relationships.

And always important is the intention behind a reading, like if you're asking for advice about a relationship to clear up tense patterns, clear needless worry or stress, or to get a confirmation that a relationship isn't serving you or someone else. In this case, reading a person who's not in the room can be helpful and healing, and often anxiety-relieving for both people. Of course, this topic is complex, but that's the gist of it.

And what if you're reading this book wondering if all the evil people will read it and then use it to know more about you? Uh, well, I have to say that some of the most malicious and manipulative people I've met in my life were also ridiculously intuitive. So why don't we all get good at this skill and use it for happy-feeling, well-intended things? Ill intent usually stems from a deep-down feeling of powerlessness. And what's one way to feel empowered? To be able to trust your inner compass.

But let's say you get tons of information about other people and really badly want to dish out everything you know and tell everyone how to fix themselves in order to heal the world? Don't. Please. First, as I said already, they won't like it. Second, they may not be ready for your message and won't be able to truly hear what you've got to say. Third, you may be robbing them of the opportunity to learn the lesson on their own time and therefore they'll lose out on gaining valuable life skills. Fourth, there's probably a hidden message in there about what you need to learn. So, it's best to turn the lens in on yourself. Where the mind goes, energy flows, and if you're focused on someone else, you're essentially leaking precious energy you could be using to heal yourself.

Rob & Bob & Friday Night

I was out on a Friday night when I bumped into a sensitive friend — let's call him Rob. I was hanging out with another sensitive friend — let's call him Bob — and we were en route to go dancing. Bob met Rob, they started walking together, and I sped up ahead. I was minding my own business, checking out the scene, when I got the image of a volcano about to erupt. I looked behind me and noticed Bob and Rob in a heated debate. I couldn't hear them, but images started popping out at me: Bob looked small and red, his aura crackling and spitting, as I saw the image of a tall, white-haired man with a whistle and Polo tee behind Rob. He looked like a football coach or something — offensive, bullying. I waited for them to catch up to me and heard Rob telling Bob something about an inability to open his heart. Bob looked hurt. But I said nothing, did nothing, not knowing what to do actually because...well, three psychics all reading each other for no good reason on a Friday night just felt like a mess.

"What are you guys talking about?" I managed to say. Rob ignored me, continued talking at Bob, doing what seemed like a reading. Bob looked hurt, Rob looked tense and, well, the ghosty, white-haired guy floating in the ether behind

Rob was just...there. What's funny was, knowing Rob just a bit, it sounded like he was describing himself. And as for the image behind his head...well, for all I know he could've been talking about a total stranger or mimicking one or acting out the energy of his own wounds from long ago...let's just say there were a lot of layers. Finally, everyone got silent and so I grabbed Bob and we hurried away.

When we finally hit the dance floor, he perked up. And so I asked him what happened, "I don't know...Rob just started telling me all this stuff all of a sudden...and I felt so...so judged." He looked nauseous. "Did he ask you first?" Bob shook his head and a tear rolled down his cheek. I gave him a hug and we danced it off.

Seeing how much an uninvited reading had hurt my friend reminded me why never to share impressions unless asked. (And definitely not on a Friday night when there's dancing to be done!) Seeing all those extra images, especially of that strange man, made me question what the whole thing was about. I share this story to share my belief that there's an appropriate time and place for all of this — just because you can read others doesn't mean it's helpful to do so. In fact, in social situations, it can be unhelpful and inaccurate, not to mention hurtful. Of course, as a sensitive person, I know all too well that sometimes impressions come without our inviting them, without our being able to tell the difference between a "knowing" and what's actually said, without our understanding that they are, in fact, impressions, that sometimes we speak of them without knowing what we've done. This psychic thing has sometimes felt like owning laser fingers without having been taught how to aim them. Learning how to read others in a conscious way changed all that. In the past, in situations like the one with Rob and Bob, I may not have been able to separate out all the different parts I was "seeing," I may not have been able to hold my tongue, but understanding the difference between my physical reality and my energetic impressions has changed my life.

And what if you have no idea what I'm making a big deal about, but are now wondering if I might be seeing things? And if you can start to see things too? Sure! Let's get this started.

Does this EVER Happen to You? If so...

a Quick & Easy ENeRGy CLeaNSe :

gold
Neutral
eNeRgy
(like a showeR!)

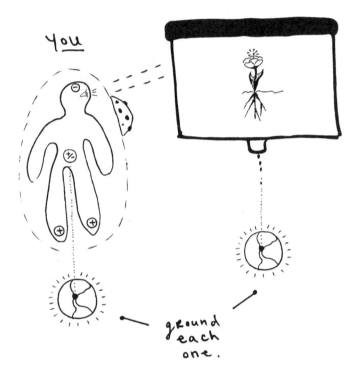

ENERGY TOOL #9:
Flower Reading For Other People (Even Pets!)

By now, you've got tons of good practice for how to open a reading and set the space — through Plugging In, Calling Back Energy, Creating a Separation Object, Centering, Reading Yourself, Connecting to Guides and Angels, and more! After we get into this tool, we'll talk about the all-important part of Closing and Clearing after a reading — even an accidental Friday night one — so make sure you've got some time.

Remember, before reading for anyone, get permission. Did I stress the importance of permission? Just kidding. Pretty sure I did. And it's also useful to read in a quiet, private space. If you're reading long-distance, via phone or Facetime, make sure your readee — AKA the person you're reading — is also in a quiet, private space, so you're not accidentally reading something or someone else. Read with your eyes closed so you can easily focus on subtle energies, rather than putting unnecessary effort into tuning out what's going on in your physical world.

To Open: Connect With Your Spirit Team & Set Intentions

I always ask for guidance from Archangels Michael, Metatron, Raphael, and Gabriel for feelings of safety, healing, and clear communication, along with my team of guides and any other qualities of higher guidance energy that present themselves for the reading. I set an intention to learn something and to help my readee and myself (because we're always helping each other during reading) for the good of all beings everywhere. You can use this one or set an even more specific and personal intention, of course!

STEP 1: Run Your Basic Energy Tools

Release your old Grounding Cord and create a new one, to signify that you're in a new moment. Plug in to Earth and Cosmic Energy. Center and feel your

Core Channel, your Separation Object, programming it with what you want to interact with — for example love and understanding. Feel your own auric space.

STEP 2: Read Yourself

Do a quick read of yourself, so you can be aware of your own space and your own energy before you invite someone else into the reading. (This has the added bonus of working your clair-senses!)

STEP 3: Create a Space for Energy Reading

A. Imagine a screen out in front of you, beyond the edges of your subtle energy body, so it's clear you're reading energy outside of your own space. Give the screen its own Grounding Cord. If you can't "see" it, just set the intention by pretending, until one day you do — both work :)

B. Imagine a clear glass rose on it.

C. Ask your readee to say their own full name three times, so you're connecting to their energy through voice. Allow their essence to fill the rose.

D. Sit back, relax, and watch with your mind's eye as the rose starts to develop some character. Then, just say what you see. Describe out loud its leaves, petals, color, density, roots, crown, soil, the flowers surrounding it, how it's growing. Is it upright? Bent to one side? Wilted? Full of petals? Still? Moving? Tall? Short? What else do you notice yourself wanting to say about the rose? Do your best not to interpret, only to call out exactly what you see. This might take a sec when you're first starting, so just be patient!

*NOTE: When you first start reading, it's easier if your readee stays silent so you can focus on what you're seeing, like describing a dream. Give yourself at least 10 minutes to watch and describe as the rose changes form, as your camera lens shifts and shows you different angles, areas, and perspectives. A flower or plant really serves as a beautiful metaphor for us humans — close enough so we can understand, but far enough away so we can get a more neutral reading. Something that may not mean much to us can be powerfully symbolic to another. So, don't be shy, and say all of what you see!

To Close: We'll get to this in a sec...first, a love story!

(And then see Energy Tool #10 – Closing a Reading.)

...And as always, if you like, write about your reading here!

write!

_____

_____

_____

_____

_____

Justine & Her Crush

A few years ago, I was at a festival when one of my friends — let's call her Justine — fell in love. All night, she gushed over a guy she'd spent the day with, a guy from a band we'd seen earlier that day, a guy who, even just standing there doing nothing, kinda creeped me out. But because she was so lovey-eyed, I kept it to myself. I was sure he was totally wrong for her, and later that weekend, when her love affair went south and she was in tears, I couldn't hold back anymore. "I knew there was something not right about that guy! How dare he mess with you! And — " Thankfully a psychic sister who was sitting with us interrupted what might've been a totally pointless rant and suggested we do a reading. We set the space, called in our guides, and asked for help with healing the relationship so our friend could rest well that night. Then we began to read.

As soon as I tuned in, I burst out laughing — not only did this guy's "flower" look exactly like mine, but when it came to romance, we both shared the same destructive pattern. He looked wilted and bent over from having spent too much of his energy on trying to please Justine, and suddenly I wanted to hug the guy. Well, his flower. And myself. What the reading showed me was the guy really did mean well, but he'd been over-giving in relationships to the point of exhaustion. This, at the time, was something I could not stand about myself. No wonder I thought I didn't like him. When I looked at him, I saw everything I didn't want to face about myself. In the end, not only did the reading help our friend have an honest conversation with this truly lovely man (and help her see she was choosing unavailable guys), but it also helped me learn how to go easier on myself.

Matching Pictures, Healing Through Reading

Generally, when we feel either a strong attraction to someone (in Justine's case) or totally repelled by that person (in mine), it's because we share what some psychic schools refer to as a "matching picture." This simply means we have something, some pattern, in common. If we really like a vibe or trait we share, we might really like the person. On the other hand, if it's a behavior we can't stand about ourselves — especially one we don't want to admit to — we will probably think we don't like the person at all. And that's because like attracts like in energy.

Have you ever sat next to a total stranger, only to realize you have so much in common? Like you have the same love of tiny flute playing, went to the same kindergarten, or your grandparents were from the same town? Have you been walking through a busy city and saw the same person among thousands again and again? That's because like attracts like in energy. And in reading, we refer to this as having "Matching Pictures," or matching gifts, likes and dislikes, patterns, and even wounds.

As I mentioned, when we perceive with our five senses, we look for differences to give us information — for instance, the texture of metal vs. wood will tell you what you're touching — and with energy, we perceive what's the same. Why? Because when reading energy, we can't understand the energetic pattern of something we haven't experienced. For instance, how can you spot the color blue if you've never seen it? How can you know you've come across sadness if you've never felt it before or recognize the taste of strawberry if you'd never eaten one? And how would you know the energetic constitution of a love story gone wrong or a rough break-up if you've never split with anyone in a way that was totally heart-wrenching? You couldn't. The image of a weird old white-haired man kind of bullying your friend? You get it.

Anyway, I freaking LOVE this about energy reading, because it means consciously looking for similarities between ourselves and others. In other words, we can look at other humans through the lens of compassion, understanding what, between you and I, is the same. So, basically, whatever you see in someone else... ditto. If you see a beautiful quality in someone, chances are you have it. If there's something you can't stand about someone, well, you'd better take a look at yourself in the mirror and love all your parts, my friend, because you are likely vibrating at that frequency too. In this case, how do you tell your stuff from someone else's? There's no difference, even though the similarity between your stuff and someone else's isn't always obvious. But that's why reading others, learning about all you see, can ultimately be very healing.

And this is where I also get confused with the question we sensitives and empaths have about feeling other people's "stuff." Because, with this logic (and as I've seen), there is no such thing as someone else's — we choose how much we want to engage with certain energies. For instance, just because you know sadness doesn't mean you have to become a counselor for someone else's grief. You'd likely do better to work on your own. But I will say this is a question with a grey area type of answer.

One of my editors told me about the time she took up tarot reading when she was falling in love, and everyone's reading seemed to be about falling in love. And then she was still reading tarot as she was breaking up, and everyone's reading seemed to be about breaking up. She said it made her quit tarot, which is a shame, because this is simply a question of matching pictures. It's likely that the people she attracted were vibrating a similar relationship energy that she was. Getting a good read on yourself before reading anyone else, making sure to center before you cast out your focus (your metaphoric fishing line), will help give clarity on these sorts of situations. And paying attention to this stuff will alert us when we're about to take on an energy, or in more Earthly terms, try to walk in someone else's shoes or solve a problem for them when it might benefit us to solve our own stuff.

Ultimately, working with matching pictures is useful — in reading and in daily life. Not only does it mean you will likely be able to do a more accurate read, or get to know yourself better, but it can also be very healing. Most of us are harder on ourselves than on anyone else. But if we can see a trait in someone else and find compassion for them, or at least see how they can get over their problem or difficult pattern, it means we can also overcome or accept the "matching picture" in ourselves. In the reading tool below, we'll add a step to close a reading by clearing out matching pictures. By doing this, you're acknowledging what you learned from the reading and setting the intention to let go and transform old experiences and teachings you've had. And that is helpful for composting the energy that you're ready to be done with.

Reflections, Matching Pictures

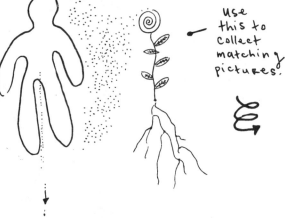

ENERGY TOOL #10:
Closing A Reading

When reading for someone else, you always want to make sure to close your reading so you can go about your day aligned with your own energy and your readee with theirs. Ultimately, we each have to walk our own path. And remember, when you allow others to walk theirs, you're sending the message, "I trust and I believe in you," which is, in itself, a very healing statement and frequency. So...

To Close: **Get Feedback, Thank Your Guides, Release Matching Pictures, Call Back Your Energy**

Technically, there's no opening, since you'll be doing this at the end of a reading. BUT if you want to make a ritual of this when you find yourself needing this tool in daily life — for instance, after an accidental Friday night reading or because you've noticed you've got some matching pictures with a friend — think or speak out loud the intention to clear matching pictures.

STEP 1: Get Feedback

While practicing, ask for feedback on the symbols you "saw" and how they related to what the readee felt you could "see." Getting feedback helps to start developing your energetic library AND further validates your super psychic self in order to build self-trust!

STEP 2: Release Matching Pictures

Use a new clear glass rose and spiral it around your energy body — either through reading it visually or feeling it around your physical body — setting the intention for it to absorb anything you've seen and are ready to release. Then, visualize burying and composting it into the center of the Earth. By doing this, you're helping to heal yourself and release old wounds through setting the intention to release what you've now seen and are done with!

STEP 3: Get Present & Release the Reading

A. Declare the reading complete, out loud. Thank your guides, angels, and ancestors. A nice way to complete is to say something like, "Thank you for this reading, I now declare it complete and trust in the perfection of what was shared. I bless you on your own path, and me on mine."

B. Visualize, feel, or sense in some other way, your current Grounding Cord releasing and create a new one.

C. Use Energy Tool #2 and call back your own energy so you can feel energized, walking your own path for the rest of the day! Take a few minutes to breathe, feel your body, and come back to yourself. If you're excited about the reading, take a few minutes to feel into that so you can give yourself time to come back to yourself. And, totally optional: Dance! Because when is that not fun? If you're having trouble disconnecting, you can tap on your own body, all the way down to your feet, talk to yourself, or even look at yourself in the mirror. Also optional:

write!

_____
_____
_____
_____

...How do you feel when you *know* you've disconnected?

write!

_____

_____

_____

_____

draw!

Say What You See, A Note On Interpretation

When you did your reading, did you notice you wanted to give advice or interpret the information you got? Sorry to say, but...if you did, don't. As you may know from life (and from Chapter 4), we all have filters. And when beginning to read for others, you have to get a lot of practice to get to know your own filters — which is excellent for helping to clear them, mind you! Remember, we are complex creatures, with heaps of different experiences, and because of that, we can misinterpret things, especially when beginning to read. While I might assume a friend's not calling me back because she's too busy to talk to me, she might not be calling me back because she wants to seem too busy to talk to me because someone was mean to her in 2nd grade for not being busy enough. Life's complicated. So, when beginning to read for others, just say what you see — by communicating your own experience of images, words, sensations — so you'll act as a mirror for your readee and allow their own internal system of guidance to direct them.

Here's the difference: Let's say a picture to do with busy-ness comes up in a reading. It's better to say something like, "I see an image of a person doing ten things" or "my body seems pulled in ten directions and I feel anxious" rather than something like "it seems like you're too busy and you should probably slow down." Sharing impressions like the first two develops your skill for sensing because you're focused on the details of what you're "seeing" and it has the added bonus of allowing your readee to share feedback on your impressions, which helps both of you! Being objective and simply saying what you see helps avoid misinterpretation when reading others or yourself when receiving your own intuitive guidance daily.

Stage Fright: What If Nothing Came At All?

What if it feels like you got no impressions at all? This happens to the best of us. Sometimes we don't get much because the person we're reading doesn't want to be read. This happened in one of my workshops where a computer engineer came to open his intuitive mind, yet admitted that he didn't believe much in this stuff. Of course, he couldn't read or be read. And when my super psychic energy reader friend couldn't read him, all he said was, "I'm having trouble reading." Which was exactly what was going on for the man. Opening up to something new takes faith, trust, and a whole lot of vulnerability. In reading, we're learning to trust ourselves fully, and therefore must be willing to make mistakes. Reading energy, especially for a total stranger whom you know nothing about, is also an exercise in humility. It's kind of like trusting that if you fall, there will not just be someone there to catch you, but there must also be a perfect reason for having fallen in the first place. And what if you don't see visuals? Well, this story's a great example of why you might as well just say out loud what you're getting – even if it means not much to you or the message is "I'm having trouble getting clarity" – you can see how accurate my friend really was! And, this way, you let the person you're reading fill in the blanks for themselves and see that there's a shared experience in it. Guaranteed, it will have more meaning for them that way and allow them to come to their own insights and clarity, which is empowering for everyone involved.

Advanced Topics in Energy Reading

9.

Petra & Her Pet Fish

So...about that time I read a goldfish. I was reading for a friend and fellow psychic when she interrupted to tell me that one of her pet fish had died. She was really choked up about it, worried that the other one — who seemed to be swimming funny ever since the incident — was about to follow the same fate. She asked if I wouldn't mind reading for her pet goldfish. I paused because at that point, I'd never read a fish before. I told her so, but she asked if I could give it a try anyway. And so with her help, I set up my reading space, reeled in my focus and cast it out again at her little pet fish. And I'll be honest when I say that I was totally surprised, if not a little shocked, when right away I saw the image of a pH strip, and some badly colored water. And when I shared it, of course, she said she'd been having trouble with the filter in her tank but had thought it was all fixed. She thanked me for the information and we got off the phone.

A few weeks later, she texted to say she'd taken that tank in, and sure enough, there'd been a problem with the filtration system. But now it was fixed and her fish lived. Now, I can't say I'm going to make a career out of pet fish reading, but it taught me that really, we can read anything if we try. It's simply about intention.

On Intention

So if you were paying attention, and giving yourself credit, chances are that at this point in your new psychic reading career, you're starting to get some good intuitive hits. And what was the difference between reading ourselves, our surroundings, and now reading for others? A change of focus, and therefore intention. In one chapter, we made a clear decision to read ourselves; in another, we shifted focus to our environment. In the last chapter, we changed it again. Easy. All we had to do was redirect our intention, which means that where we choose to focus our energy says lots about what we perceive.

If we go back to the story of Amber and her rotten egg from waaaay back in Chapter 2 and ask, How did she know the rotten egg was referring to her rotten relationship? Well, she was focused on that one thing in that moment, so when her answer came, there was no question what it was about. The more deeply you get into reading, you'll see intention is the key to it all.

If you intend to read your own energy or the energy of a situation, as we'll get to in a sec, you must be wholeheartedly focused on it. And it works the other way too. If you notice you're getting random information, for instance, about another person not liking you, that's a helpful signal letting you know what you've set your sights on. (And as an added bonus, you can shift your focus if it's hurting rather than helping you.) It's kind of like reeling in your fishing line to cast it out again in the direction you want, or turning up the volume on the part of a song you really like. And it's cool, because it means we can read the situation of anything by simply setting an intention!

Here are a few easy tools for reading the situations that tend to stump us the most in life. Practicing with these, you can not only help our friends, but you can sharpen your intuition when it comes to situations that come up from day to day. The following are some of my favorites for relationships, career stuff, and planning future dates. Enjoy!

Reading Relationships ♡

So let's build on all our reading tools with a fun one for relationships! As humans, we're always in a relationship with other people and things, whether we like it or not. So learning to read the energy of relationships is helpful, fun, and you can learn a lot about yourself while you're at it. It is one of THE most useful tools I have.

When you're reading a relationship, you'll usually be reading the pattern of your readee and how they are conducting themselves in the relationship, so this isn't about snooping into a random third person's energy field. Here's an example: If you're in a monogamous relationship and suspect your partner's cheating — rather than look at if he or she is cheating — it's so much more helpful to look at the reason why you're not trusting them or why you're choosing unfaithful partners in the first place. Reading in that way will help clear filters, or in other words, shift a belief or behavior pattern to make sure it doesn't keep coming around!

The first time I ever read a relationship, I only saw one thing: two flowers furiously trying to outgrow each other — competing, in a sense. I was a bit nervous to share the image, but as soon I did, my readee told me she was going through a divorce. She then asked if I saw that she would stay with her man. While I didn't feel comfortable answering that sort of question for her — because really, we all have choices — I asked instead to be shown what it was that would create a more harmonious relationship between them. Soon, I watched as her flower shrank, and his moved next to hers and hugged hers from above. Now, if we *were* going to interpret that image, it would seem that in order for them to stay together, she'd have to shrink herself, and at that point, he'd be more affectionate. Of course, I only shared the picture with her, what the flowers showed. She thanked me for the information, and said it did feel like her and her husband were always trying to out-do each other. I never got feedback on whether or not they'd decided to stay together after all, but she did get very serious and silent after I shared what I saw, and I can only assume it was at that point that her own clarity and insight kicked in about what to do.

ENERGY TOOL #11

Relationships sometimes...

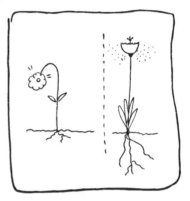
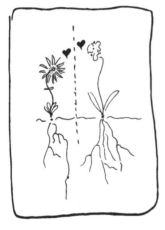
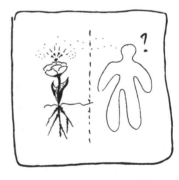

...How do the flowers interact?

ENERGY TOOL #11:
Flower Reading For Relationships

Sometimes it's hard to get an objective read on our own relationships, since relationship patterns are so closely tied to survival. Because of this, it's so super helpful to practice this one by reading relationships for other people first, especially ones that don't impact you so much. That way, you can get to know your filters and blind spots when it comes to relationships before you start reading your own. Once you get some practice, you can use this tool for so many things! You can get helpful insight on anything from romance to office politics and even group dynamics. I recommend starting with this basic recipe first, then get creative with it once you've got it down.

To Open: Set up Your Reading Tools, Call in Guides, Set an Intention

You know this by now! Call in your team for spiritual guidance and say your intention out loud or to yourself.

STEP 1: Run Your Basic Energy Tools

Release your old Grounding Cord and create a new one. Plug in to Earth and Cosmic Energy. Center and feel your Core Channel, your Separation Object, programming it with what you want to interact with — like love and connection. Feel your own auric space.

STEP 2: Read Yourself

Do a quick read of yourself, so you can be aware of your own space and your own energy before you invite other energies into the reading. (Work those clair-senses!)

STEP 3: Create a Space for Energy Reading

A. Imagine a screen out in front of you, beyond the edges of your subtle energy body, so it's clear that you're reading energy outside of your own space. Give the screen its own Grounding Cord.

B. Imagine two clear roses — one on the left side of the screen, one on the right.

C. Ask your readee to say their own full name three times, so you're connecting to their energy through voice. Allow their essence to fill one rose first. Watch what it does for 1 minute.

D. Ask your readee to say the full name of the other person just once, to get an impression of the relationship, while still primarily focused on your readee. Allow the other person's essence to fill the other rose.

E. Watch and describe how the two flowers interact — do they look the same size? Shape? Color? Are they pulling toward one another or away? Are there certain parts of the flowers that are closer than others? What do you feel in your body while reading? Expansive? Heart-fluttery? Attracted? Repelled? Small? Is there another energy in the mix that wants to make itself known? And if so, where is it?

*BONUS: Ask inwardly, what would create the most harmonious picture? Continue to allow it to unfold for 10 minutes as more information is revealed and just say what you see!

To Close: Announce the Reading Complete, Thank Your Guides, Ask for Feedback, Call Back Your Energy

Yup! Energy Tool #10. You got this!

...When you first start reading relationships, be super extra cautious to say only what you see. Many of us hold onto lots of beliefs, anxious patterns, and false filters when it comes to relationships. Because of this, I find that at first it helps to read without your subject asking questions, and then have them ask questions later on — many times you'll see that you've already answered their questions with a general energy read!

write!

_____
_____
_____
_____
_____

Asking Good Questions

So you might've noticed that I creeped a little question into this reading tool — what would create the most harmonious picture? As you get more confident with reading, you're going to want to start directing your focus. And in order for the reading to be most helpful to both you and your readee, you want to direct your focus by asking good questions.

For those of you already steeped in tarot and other intuitive practices, you probably know there's an art to asking good questions, using specific language for what you're ultimately wanting as the end goal. Here are some examples to build on:

- What would bring feelings of peace and _____ to this situation?

- What about this relationship pattern creates a feeling of _____?

- What am I not seeing about _____ that would be helpful for me to know?

- How can I best help _____? What is best said and left unsaid?

- What would be most helpful to focus on in this reading about _____?

- What are next steps for today? Tomorrow? A month from now?

- Is there a mantra, practice, or other type of solution that would be good to know about or share?

...Now, try asking some of these questions for your next reading, and see how it shifts what you see or sense. Journal about it on the next page!

ENERGY tool #12

Like Relationships but... with a desk!

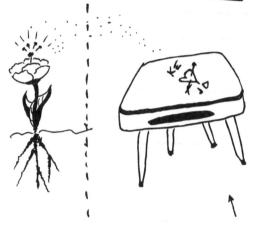

this "WORK" desk looks like a school desk... is there something you need to learn still at your work?

...Keep on saying what you see.

ENERGY TOOL #12:
Career Reading

Some of the questions I get asked the most are about relationships and careers, so here's a tool that builds on what we've already done that shows how you can read all sorts of things simply by shifting your intention!

To Open: Set up Your Reading Tools, Call in Guides, Set an Intention

Yup! Call in your team for spiritual guidance and say your intention out loud or to yourself. Maybe for this one, you'll want to be clear about whether you're looking for a career that supports survival needs, a sense of purpose, or a mixture of both!

STEP 1: Run Your Basic Energy Tools

Release your old Grounding Cord and create a new one. Plug in to Earth and Cosmic Energy. Center and feel your Core Channel, your Separation Object, programming it with the energy you want to interact with — for example, love and support. Feel your own auric space.

STEP 2: Read Yourself

Do a quick read of yourself, so you can be aware of your own space, your own energy before you invite other energies into the reading. (Work those clair-senses!)

STEP 3: Create a Space for Energy Reading

A. Imagine a screen out in front of you, beyond the edges of your subtle energy body, so it's clear that you're reading energy outside of your own space. Give the screen its own Grounding Cord.

B. Imagine a clear glass rose **or stick** figure to represent you or another person — yes, we're getting **advanc**ed now!

C. Ask your readee (which could be you!) to say their own full name three times, so you're connecting **to their** energy through voice. Allow that essence to fill a rose first. **Watch** what it does for 1 minute and then...

D. Move that picture to one side of the screen and have your subject (which, again, could be you!) ask a question about their career, and create a desk (a symbol **that speaks** to many of us about work and projects) on the other side. If you're not visual, feel into your right side, which for most of us, represents doing work-related things. Now, say what you see, sense, or feel. Here are some good questions to ask:

- How do the two energies interact? Are they animated? Does the desk become big and seem overwhelming next to the flower? Is it pretty and comfy and does it match nicely with the person's energy?

- How is the flower's posture near the desk?

- How far away are the two?

- Are they facing toward or away from each other?

- Does one figure seem to be in the back or front of the screen, as opposed to left or right? For me, this always relates to the situation being in the past or future.

- Are there cords, obstacles, other energies between them? If so, where?

- What does the background look like? What's the overall vibe?

- What creates the most harmonious picture?

E. Watch and describe, giving yourself at least 10 minutes as the rose shifts form, as your camera lens shifts and shows you different angles, areas and perspectives, sharing your results, like describing a dream. The scenario might even shift into something totally new!

To Close: **Announce the Reading Complete, Thank Your Guides, Ask for Feedback, Call Back Your Energy**

Yup! Energy Tool #10. And for fun, get up and dance!

*BONUS: Other Fun Things to Try!

· Read the energy of a hobby project vs. work. How do they look similar? Different?

· Read the energy of a relationship with a coworker using your tool for Relationship Reading. How does the reading look the same? Different?

· Read the energy of another situation, swapping out the desk for a vacation plan — you can use an airplane or a location on a map! Or ask another burning question...so many options!

...How did this compare to other types of reading? Write about it here!

write!

_____

_____

_____

_____

ENERGY TOOL LUCKY #13:
Psychic Reading — Predictions & Time

Time lines and dates can be useful in readings, and I personally love to know which ones will be extra-important for me. Knowing something will happen that I'm very much looking forward to puts my mind at ease. As does knowing the perfect time to take a trip, book a meeting, or stay home. When reading others, this tends to be useful for couples wanting to get pregnant, in which case a baby spirit will often pop into the picture and show a date for when a readee will meet a partner, heal a block, conceive, or give birth. It's pretty cool!

Don't be shy about this. Anyone can do a psychic reading! If you can sense energy (and we've been practicing this all along) then you can take the temperature, so to speak, of what's to come. Remember that thought creates form, ideas become creations, and if you can sense the energy of thoughts, ideas, and the passion that sparks them into being...well, you know what's going to come! Personally, I "see" trajectories of energy that are currently taking up space in someone's field, ready to be brought into being. Dates pop out at me, or if I visualize a clock or calendar, certain times seem to have weight to them, messages about what's blocking these things from being born feel like a tap on my head. And these things come through in a different way for everyone. So you might as well try it and see how it shows up for you! When doing this, remember you have the power to choose your beliefs. Therefore, nothing you see is set in stone, so you can generally adjust your own trajectory of energy. That's why it's helpful to know where your energy is headed, like steering a boat, so you can make a decision to turn the ship if you want!

This tool is sort of a creative take on classic Remote Viewing techniques that I rediscovered as I was searching for a new creative outlet and picked up a pen. In between writing and whatever else I was doing, I was waiting for a text about my schedule for the day. I let my hand doodle freely and before I gave it much thought, I'd sketched out a clock with the hands pointed to 11:43. And guess what happened when the clock struck that time? I got my text, of course. I'd asked a question in my head and channeled the answer through my pen. If you allow yourself to do it, the results are surprising. And useful! Now you try...

To Open: Call in Your Guides

That's it. We're going to do this one a little differently.

STEP 1: Just Go for It!

A. Write your question at the top of a piece of paper.

B. Get into your meditative space, plug in your energy, center yourself.

C. Let your pen in hand dance over the page — even if all that comes are squiggles. Time yourself for at least 12 minutes, so you have a chance to tune in.

D. At the end, study your drawing and free-write some conclusions at the bottom of the page to finish.

If you just squiggled lines, here are some things to consider: What do your lines look like? Are they harsh and boxed in? Flowing? Easy? Tense? Moving down or otherwise upward? What are some images you drew? Letters? Do they remind you of anything? Recall memories?

To Close: Get Present in Your Body

Release your Grounding Cord and create a new one for the present moment, thank your guides, and get up and dance. While our mind and our energy can be anytime, anywhere, our body is always in the present moment, so...to get present, use your body!

*BONUS: Other Fun Things to Try!

• Try scribbling words instead of pictures and see which words you accidentally messed up, scribbled over, made bold, or underlined.

• Try making abstract pencil marks and see if they tell you more than when you try to draw figures.

• Try doing this without looking at the page!

...If you want this exercise to be more about time lines, work with drawing an actual calendar — daily, monthly, yearly — and see where your hand goes when you close your eyes and center. Eventually, you can merge this with other reading tools by putting your flower or stick figure into a time line in your mind's eye.

Channeling

Let's switch the focus over to channeling for a sec — just for fun and to flex your intuitive muscles. And since the last tool was technically one for channeling (hehe surprise) you've already done it! Humans, with our insatiable need to create, are excellent channels. Even if you once made dinner without instructions, you were technically channeling a recipe. The word "channel" simply refers to bringing something from one place to another. And, if you've ever brought an idea to physical form, you could say you were channeling it. So, if you know you can already do it, and it really ain't no thing, then let's get into channeling useful guidance, shall we?

The important question is: What source are you getting your channeled information from? In the old sense of the word, we tend to think of a channel as someone who's in touch with another source, allowing it to come through them. And while this certainly falls into the category of channeling, it doesn't mean that only special people can do it or that you have to reach for a far-away and mysterious source of information. Or that you even have to allow any foreign energy into your body at all. Throughout most of this book, we've been reading by taking a look at energy that is close to us, and you can do that here too.

Personally, I like to use my gift for channeling to ask specific questions to mentors I look up to. For instance, I'd channel wisdom from an artist I admire if I need help with sculpting. And then when I move about my day, I will release them, since they may not be as good at relationships, bill paying or grocery shopping, and anyway, for those things, I'm going to want to channel myself.

What we're usually drawn to, when we get excited by a person who channels, is their ability to tap certain sources — for instance, Akashic Record libraries, baby spirits, ascended masters, and more! Really, it's just a question of where your interest lies and where you put your focus and intention. Of course, there is some Earthly knowledge required if you're going to channel, say, an old Mayan medicine woman, because you're going to want to know what she's referring to. Or if you want to become a medical medium, you're probably going to want to study all about body parts. Still, it's more accessible than you might think.

Akashic Records & Life Purpose

Reading of the akashic records is meant to help us better understand our own soul's journey over many lifetimes. It can help you understand your spiritual life purpose here on Earth right now, in this lifetime. And it's a very deep, personal, and exciting thing to connect to. Reading the akashic records is just like energy reading or channeling, only you're connecting to a very specific source to get information. And it's easier to consult the akashic records if you learn to do it directly from someone who's already strongly connected to it — almost like having a human guide lead you there — so see my website for resources. It's ultimately fun to look at your own records and to do it in meditation at times you feel you need the insight.

When you have that soul urging to do something more purposeful than what you're currently doing, it can feel so frustrating. Life purpose is not always how we think of it, especially in the West. For instance, your purpose could be something like spreading joy and smiles about the little things in life, rather than, say, being a locksmith. So, when I have felt stuck in the past, I've asked for an image — like a lucky charm or totem — to guide me. Sometimes it's a smile, a heart, a pen, or a pottery wheel, and other times it has been much more specific, like the title for a creative project.

Try this: Ask for a symbol, sign, or sensation in the body that will help guide you to people, places, and situations that can shed light on your life purpose. Let's say you feel a little ping in your pinky finger when you do this. Well, you'll know that your little pinky might lead you down the path of your purpose then. I have a specific series of numbers that leads me to mine. See what comes up for you!

Baby Spirits

Just like you can tap into ancestors of the past by simply shifting your intention, you can tap into ancestors of the future too. In the spirit world, time doesn't exist, and babies are simply spirits. I often find myself sitting randomly next to someone who's just lost someone, someone who has a sick pet, or someone who's trying to conceive, because the spirits of these beings must know I can connect with them. And I bring this up because it seems to be a matter of what we're open to. So, if you want to connect with baby spirits, announce out loud right now that you're open to it!

Baby spirits can usually be seen circling around someone who's really wanting a baby. And it's super helpful to tap in — for one thing, to take the pressure off. Baby spirits can help lead you to your mate if you're single, simply by virtue of them wanting to come into this world with a specific set of parents and lessons to be learned. Yes, I know this sounds contrary to much of what we've been taught, but I've seen them time and again next to friends who've got baby on the brain, those who only *think* they're having trouble getting pregnant. After all, if baby is coming in to learn a specific lesson, then sometimes it can take some time for those conditions to be right, for a mother's body to prepare for that always perfect timing.

I've found that many mothers-to-be already know much about their babies-to-be when they allow themselves permission to talk to their baby spirits — try it! If it feels uncomfortable or strange while awake, ask for communication in your dream-space. As with anything, make sure to plug in your energy, call in your guides and angels, maybe even ancestors for this one, for help with navigating the spirit plane and connecting to family, past and future.

Ascended Masters, Mentors & "Trying On" Energy

Have you ever felt really stuck in life, thinking that only other people can do something, but not you? And yet, you'd really like to be able to do that thing? When we feel jealous of other people, usually this is what's beneath it — we see them having something we want, but for some deep down reason, we think we can't. You know what's a really quick way to fix that? Call in a specific quality of energy, so you can "see" or "feel" what it's like to have what you want. Of course, there are teachers in physical form, but energy patterns can teach us so much too! Do you want to know what it's like to feel in love? Try calling up images or sounds from an old romantic movie. Do you want to walk with confidence no matter what? Call up imagery of your favorite superhero and, in your mind's eye, try on her or his clothes!

When I first started writing, I thought I wasn't good enough, and so I called on the energy of an author I love who's in spirit for a little confidence, inspiration, and help. Even to this day, sometimes I still ask him to stand behind me as I write. When I'm feeling ungrounded (as airy fairies sometimes do), I'll look to someone in the physical world who seems to have the type of groundedness I'd like to have — I ask to see an image of it in my mind's eye, and feel what it feels like in my body for a moment. For instance, one of my energy teachers looks, to me, like a redwood. And when I'm feeling like I need the support, I ask for the image or sensation of a redwood to appear — try it!

Here's how: Run your energy and read someone you admire. When you do, sit with it for a moment and see what you sense in yourself! Maybe even walk around like that for a few hours. When you're done, remember to clear and call your own energy back. After all, you want to walk your own path, the one that you were uniquely put on this Earth for. No human or mentor is perfect, we all have our downfalls, and you don't want to try TOO much of someone else's stuff. For instance, maybe you want an artist's love of painting, but not their financial woes.

Letting Your Voice Go Free

Here's a fun person to channel: yourself. The truth is, we all know when we're telling the truth or lying to ourselves. Connecting to your own system of inner guidance, along with higher guides, means you can typically speak freely and may even be surprised by what comes out of your mouth! Try telling yourself a lie, such as "I hate cilantro." It won't work if you love cilantro. You will sense the dissonance in your own voice.

So, yes, I'm suggesting that you try talking to yourself more. When I'm connected and aligned, I find myself talking out loud about a forecasted date or timeline when I'm least expecting it, least attached to the outcome or answer. If this seems awkward, try it like this first: Get into your meditative space (alone), run your tools, ask a question, and just start talking. This works your skills for clairaudience — it is one of the easiest tools to use, and super fun to try out. Not to mention, it's so helpful in daily life. If you feel stuck, one way to clear the energy of honest communication (especially with yourself) is to practice singing!

Chessa & Her New Job

Well, that was a lot. Maybe you just tried your first bunch of readings and weren't sure you got any information — for some, this is a little like learning to walk. Maybe you just saw a color, a texture, felt a feeling, or had a persistent thought that seemed like it kept interrupting your readings, even though it might have very well been the topic of your reading. Sometimes, this is just about learning to trust what comes up.

I was once reading a woman in search of new career opportunities. When she asked about her perfect new job, nothing came in. I sat with it for a moment, but all I could see was an office space that looked like my friend Chessa's. I had to tell my client something, and so I just began speaking freely, "I'm having a persistent memory of my friend Chessa — she's an interior designer, but does stage design and all sorts of events too. I'm seeing her office, and she's surrounded by women all freelancing at various jobs. She looks happy to be chatting to so many unique and different women."

Of course, my client doesn't know Chessa personally, but as soon as I began, she started giggling. Turns out she was an interior designer in search of new types of events to work on, and also looking at an office space just like the one I described. So, sometimes you may get a specific memory or thought come up during a reading, and it might seem irrelevant, but in actuality, it could be your claircognizance at work. My philosophy is this: Just say what comes. So long as you're in your meditative guided space, focused on the reading, the essence of whatever comes through will almost always be just right.

taking
YOUR
Psychic Skills
to the
WORLD!

10.

Daniela & The Shapeshifter

I was sitting at a café when a friend asked if she could talk to me about something "crazy" that happened. At this point, nothing sounds weird to me and in fact, I look forward to hearing how the universe is lovingly entertaining my friends. So, Daniela had been trying to call in a long-term relationship. She'd always had an easy time meeting, but never committing, to men. She'd decided to work on shedding some of the past stuff she was holding onto when it came to relationships, and when she met Adam, she fell hard. While it was true that Adam reminded her of her last boyfriend, she figured by the time she met him that she'd done enough clearing of exes from her life and shifted her focus to Adam.

"But then we were in bed together, Court," she told me, "and...he like... literally turned into my ex!" She stopped to stare into my face for signs of disbelief, but there were none. And so she opened the floodgates: described how he felt, looked, spoke, and even smelled exactly like her ex, so much so that she'd had to back away from him a few times mid-makeout just to see if he was still Adam. Weirdly, he wasn't.

"So what do you think? What is that?" She asked. "Well, it kinda looks like you've got a human tarot card on your hands." Because here she had a big cute man-sized sign telling her she needed to do some more clearing. The next day, she decided to meet up with her ex and try to tie up loose ends. It took months, mind you, to clear a bunch of patterns and past beliefs it all dug up, but now she's in a happy relationship, and the work she did on clearing her filters was totally worth it, thanks to the sign she got from Adam.

If this story makes no sense to you...well, one day it might. The point is that as you work your senses and intuition, it becomes helpful in ways you never thought possible. And as you get creative with your Energetic Library — that is, with the signs and symbols you relate to and understand — they can show up as anything! Even as a cute and cuddly human! Remember, we can choose to learn our lessons through joy or through pain — why not choose lessons and symbols that can come through sharing love and having fun? We are truly creative beings.

So, what's next on your journey of becoming even more of the highly intuitive psychic you already are? Really just practice. And fun. But also this: What if you, like Daniela, could make the world into your very own tarot deck? What if it already is? As you continue to build your library of signs, your energy vocabulary, your arsenal of goodies and physical world tools to use along with your highly tuned intuition, every single thing you pull into your field of vision will tell you what you need to know. So, in this chapter we're going to work on building our library of symbols!

Tarot, Crystals & The World As Your Energy Library

Often, clients want to know if I'm using tarot, astrology, crystals, pendulums, and other types of tools to do my work. I don't, but tools can definitely help give structure to energy readings for those who prefer it. Because whether you're translating a tarot reading, interpreting an astrology chart, or choosing a crystal, you're using your intuition to do it.

We're all different people with different interests, unique gifts, and strengths, and so if you love your tools, there must be a good reason. My friend Aaron can calculate in an instant exactly where Neptune was at the time of your birth, and you know what? Even though he's great at doing math in his head, I notice the second he does, it sparks his creativity and his super savvy intuition — his love of astrology and its structure seems to be the thing that gets it going. So even though there's tons of math and mythology when it comes to astrology, the interpretation is a huge piece. Why? Because maybe your Sun sign is Cancer, which says you love home, comfort, and stability in relationships. But, then you also have Venus in Aries that says stability in relationships is boring. Two seasoned astrologers may look at the same chart and interpret it totally differently, depending on their life experience, their impressions of you, and the filtered lens they happen to be looking through. And so, there's a certain part of it that means using pure intuition.

And what about when you're choosing which astrologer to ask for advice, which body-worker, healer, or tarot expert to visit? You're most likely using your own intuition to do so — to guide you to who or what's going to have the information you need. You're probably going to choose someone with matching pictures — remember, like attracts like in energy. And anyway, good intuition depends on how much you trust yourself to choose a certain path — whether you're seeing answers in your mind's eye or using a tool that gives you that confidence, such as tarot decks, crystals, pendulums, coffee grinds, bones, I Ching, or any other tradition. So I say, use the tools you love and continue to work your intuition! Or even better, work it so the whole world IS your tool for clearer seeing!

Expanding Your Energy Library

One way to allow the world to be your very own tarot deck is to build up an energy library — that is, your language of signs and symbols. For instance, if I'm talking to someone and I suddenly notice my throat isn't clear, I know there's something important that's gone unspoken. If I notice a bee flying between us in a way that catches my attention, and the person responds in terror, I know it's because there's some fear of connection — bees are symbolic to me in that way. This isn't to say anytime you see a bee you should assume you're talking to a commitment-phobe — because bees are everywhere — but since this specific symbol has come up again and again in my readings and in life, I've come to recognize it as pretty reliable. Though it might sound crazy now, the world around us is quite literally a manifestation of everything in our field of vision.

Through common threads between what I see in readings and in daily life, and through recording my findings, I've developed a dialogue with my own body and the world around me. I like to think of it like keeping a dream journal, only I'm awake. For instance, the bee became an important symbol for me in waking life because I noticed that not only did it show up a lot in readings, but also in daily life; they'd show up flying oddly close to my face anytime I journaled about feeling lonely or very drawn to someone...in other words, they always appeared when I was focused hard on the subject of personal connection. When I finally googled it, I found out the bee has to do with connection in some ancient traditions too. Whether you want to develop your own symbols or work with ones that have historic significance or those you're already familiar with, it's entirely up to you. Once you have symbols established, in any shape or form, they will show up to communicate with you when you need them!

Can you think of three symbols you already use and notice in daily life? Do you have a spirit animal, favorite number, picture, song, or sign that shows up again and again? If so, write about it here!

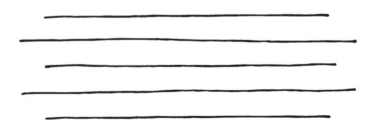

This brings me back to my point that energetic signs and symbols can literally be anything — even a beautiful make-out session with an ex, if you want to manifest it that way like Daniela did. When you decide — whether consciously or unconsciously — on what sorts of signs and symbols you're most likely to pay attention to, your energetic guidance system will present details to you in that way. For instance, I'm currently fascinated by anatomy and nature. And so, it's no wonder that signs show up as bees and plants and phantom tickles in my toe. Perhaps a bee means connection to me but danger to you, or it helps to recall the memory of a time when you felt very close to your father, who sweetly nursed a sting you got on your palm. And so, a bee is a symbol of receiving nurturing love from family. Whatever it is, when you simply make the decision to notice signs and symbols around you, choose to look deeper into the meaning of things that already recall memories. Building your own library of symbols is easy. So, let's get to it!

Exercise: Expanding Your Energy Library

We did this a little bit before, but this time we're getting detailed. Here you can expand on your library of signs and symbols, so you can get tons of help out in the world! Of course, you can be creative here and add your own words. Consider this a guide to get you started. You'll see that once you set the intention to start a library of signs and symbols, they'll start showing up everywhere. You might even be flooded with a whole bunch of memories of seeing signs and symbols out in the world right now! And if so, write them down! Again, this is sort of like keeping a dream journal, only it's about waking life. Which makes it even cooler.

Let's start with some spontaneous association. If you've been reading up until this point, you've already flexed your intuitive muscles enough to know you can trust them. And even if you're still a little wary, I ask that you please trust *me*. So, just like we've been doing this whole time, all you have to do is say what you see, say the first thing you get. If the cue is love and you see a green traffic light, well then, whenever you see a green light, and you've asked a question about love, you may want to pay attention! But, hey, you don't want to go walking into traffic just because you're looking for signs. With intuitive hits, they'll come to you, and you'll always feel a charge when they do. We'll get to that part in a minute. First...library!

To Start: This exercise is easier if you can meditate while someone calls these out to you, so either get a buddy for this (it's fun in groups!) or make yourself a voice memo with a bunch of words before you get started, and then:

1. Sit in your meditative space and run your energy.

2. Free association time again — listen to each word and see what image, body sensation, color, sound, song, or memory comes up. The first one is always the right one.

WORDS:
Relationship   Career
Friends   Hobby
Fun   Success
Flow   Money
Purpose   Message

3. To wrap up, sit with a journal and record your findings — again, like writing the details of a dream. Take 1 minute and feel into the details of each word or sensation...do you get a smell to go along with an image you saw? A taste to go along with a feeling?

*BONUS: Add your own words to the exercise above. To quickly build your library, do a word a day! And feel into the difference between similar concepts, like "relationship" vs. "friend" or "career" vs. "success" vs. "hobby," and sense the subtle differences!

Your Energy Library Out In The World

So, even though you might've started your energetic diary in a meditative space by closing your eyes and going inward, eventually you can take it to the streets! Start by noticing signs and symbols with your eyes open in your private space, and then bring it out into the world. And, you'll want to write down, as much as you can, about the different signs and symbols you see in daily life and how you interpret them, even the results you get in life after you've followed the signs. Kind of like a scientific discovery journal of your own path. It's fun!

Here's an example of what your diary entry could look like — remember, the more detailed, the easier it is to get more clear answers later, because you can look back to it for patterns and recurring themes! It's so useful.

<u>Diary Entry Example #1</u>: From a Reading...

Today I did a practice reading about relationships, here's what came up:
<u>Light blue</u> *colored energy wrapped around my* **readee's** *heart as I felt* <u>calm</u> *in my own heart. Then, the feeling changed to* <u>excitement</u> *as I saw her energy body about to make a big* <u>leap</u>, *as I thought of the concept of* <u>change</u>. *Her hand was grabbing for a cloud that was holding her energy body, and in it, she was giving herself a hug. The words "self-love" popped into my mind and I felt warm. Soon, her energy body seemed to be crawling on the earth looking for a feather. The message I "heard" then was that* <u>guidance</u> *is always around so long as she looks for the signs. I saw a* <u>feather</u>, *and as I said it, I felt* <u>tingles</u>. *When I told her about all these symbols and messages, she told me the story of her break-up, her* <u>healing</u> *process and excitement about her upcoming move - a big* <u>change</u> *for her. The symbols that really stood out from this reading were:*

Word	Symbol	Feeling
Healing	Light Blue	Calm
Change	Leap	Excitement
Guidance	Feather	Tingles

Diary Entry Example #2: From Daily Life...

Today I walked in the park, wondering about the essence of my new boss. When I did, I noticed I stopped to look at some light blue flowers, felt really calm, just when a great blue heron swooped down and landed right beside me. A thought came through just then about healing. The bird's light blue color was so similar to the flowers I was also noticing, and his feathers really stood out as my body felt tingles.

Word	Symbol	Feeling
Healing	Light Blue	Calm
Guidance	Feather	Tingles

...As you can see, there's some overlap between reading someone else's energy and reading yourself in daily life after you've asked a question. It's always great to have a base to build on. Now it's your turn!

*TO DO: Start an energy library diary, if you haven't already!

Exercise: Your Energy Library Out In The World

Sit and think about the signs and symbols you're already familiar with, so you can pull from dreams, communications with ancestors, or even times when you've noticed your favorite animal or sports team symbols popping up around you. Anything you're likely to pay attention to can be a symbol. Here are some questions to get the juices flowing:

1. Do specific themes come up in dreams? For instance, do you fly to far-off places, receive gifts and tokens in your dreams, go to school, or dream you want to run somewhere specific? Do you dream about characters or symbols or places that give you information in dreams? If so, free-write about them here — these are good clues for how your signs show up in daily life:

_____
_____
_____
_____

2. Do you have a song, symbol, or color that shows up in daily life that reminds you of a loved one who's always there to support you? See road signs that tell you which way to go (in the greater scheme of life!) when you're lost? Many of us see feathers, coins, crows, or even smell a yummy fragrance or hear a song that reminds us we're loved and guided — free-write about these things here:

_____
_____
_____
_____

3. Do you crave certain foods when certain situations come up? For instance, do you crave sweets when you're needing sweetness in your life? Chocolate when your heart needs some love? Or does your hand slip and you text certain emojis that give you good guidance and clues? Do you accidentally type, speak, or write the exact words you need to hear? Write them out now!

_____

_____

_____

_____

_____

Manifestation Vs. Confirmation

So how do you know if you can trust the signs? If you're really into manifesting, you may have noticed by now that you attract whatever you think about. And if you haven't noticed yet, you might soon. And that's when that old question might start to crop up: Can I trust it? How do I know if a synchronicity is a sign from guides and angels or just something I created to fulfill a need? Was I watching the clock and waiting for it to turn 11:11? Or is it really a sign? If so, what is it actually telling me? This tiny human doesn't have the answer to this question. All I know is as we get more powerful in our abilities to "see" the truth of all we can create in our lives, there comes a point where we can start to question who's steering the ship.

How do you know if something is "meant to be" or if you just made it so? This is where it comes in handy to have a good energy library, spiritual practice, and some tools for clearing when we need to do that. In times like these, when we're braving stormy waters, it can help us feel more stable and secure to have a strong inner compass, to feel connected to our core, our guidance; to have a language, a dialogue with it we know we can trust. I often find that when symbols crop up in daily life that have a story to tell me, I feel a very specific type of charge.

I was far away from home on some travels when I had a particularly profound night. I'd cleared a big old false filter and was feeling pretty proud of myself when I went to climb the steps to my rental. I looked ahead of me and froze. On the steps, I saw what looked like an eight-foot-long cobra. And it wasn't just any cobra, but one equipped with venom to make a human go blind. I looked at her, she looked at my shadow, and it was as if we both made the decision not to be afraid. I felt adrenaline, of course, and on top of it I felt what I refer to as my "charge"; that is, an energetic surge that rings my ears and heart like a bell when I'm being asked to pay special attention. Standing next to a being with the power to take my sight, I recognized I was now seeing more clearly. And as she started to climb the stairs, not in my shadow, but in the a spot of light, I took notice: Of her upward direction, her black and white colors, her presence at that specific moment when she crawled toward my shadow but decided not to enter it, it confirmed a very deep truth for me, and I knew what it all meant. And so, when I saw what was one of the wildest and most powerful snakes I've seen to date, I took the opportunity to climb with her. But I will say this: I'm good without snakes for a while, thanks.

At that moment, the world became my animated tarot deck, and I knew I was receiving information I needed because I'd felt a charge. Was it a manifestation or a confirmation of what I already deep down knew? Again, I'm only one tiny psychic, and I can't say for sure, but what I do know (at this moment, anyway) is in the wake of triggers and emotion and hard times, we sometimes need external confirmation that we are, in fact, on the right path, and when you walk slowly enough to observe, the world helps you through.

The Charge

So there, you can see how knowing your "charge" can bring about more clarity when you've got your library going. Because with understanding, you can quickly shift your energy. Of course, many of us might feel all charged up when faced with a wild animal, but it's also happened to me with specific desserts, mind you. I just chose the more fun story. So, what's your charge? Mine sounds like ear candy and heart bells. Do you get goose bumps, knee pain, or the feeling of weight when someone says or does something that has deeper meaning for you? What's your charge? Write about it here:

_____
_____
_____
_____

Definite Confirmation: A Sign, A Symbol

So what's the point exactly of having all these signs and symbols? Oh, just clarity, confirmation, more ease, trust, and flow in daily life. I was once chatting on the phone with a friend, telling her about a conversation I'd had that was bugging me. Stuck for answers, I talked myself in circles, so I breathed in deep, took a pause. Suddenly I realized the lesson, and made a declaration: "I think I just have to trust there was a higher purpose to that awkward conversation. I hate it, but I'm just gonna let it go." As soon as I said it, she said she got goose bumps. Then, through her phone, I heard a massive applause. I giggled. I "hear" applause from my guides when I've finally learned a lesson. Even funnier, when my friend walked by the applause, it was coming from a Jewish wedding, and the now married couple had just stomped on the glass, which is a traditional sign for luck and good fortune on a new path. In that moment, I knew I'd spoken truth because the universe responded to my statement by offering an unmistakable gift: several confirmations and symbols, even a sign for what's to come.

Exercise: Signs And Symbols In Daily Life

People always ask me if I can see their energy. The truth is, I can perceive things if I tune in, but when I'm walking about the world and relating to other people, I don't anymore. And thank goodness! Perceiving more than necessary is distracting, and reading other people when they're not sharing via actions or words can cause confusion. In fact, when I notice I'm picking up more information than is useful to me, I use it as a cue to pull my energy back in.

But of course, I do need help and guidance, as every human who walks this Earthly path does, and so I choose how I'd like my signs, symbols and other communication to show up — and I choose it in objects, words, or animals, for instance, rather than trying to get information from reading a person. Personally, I'd rather have my feet take me where I need to go, read words, and see objects that exist in real time. That way, I can still be present. And if I need extra information, I can always look to my inner space when I'm in private. Out in the world, I'd rather be embodied.

How would you like more signs and symbols to show up in the world? Set an intention! For example, maybe you're done with getting your info through other people and would much rather get your signs through shuffling your music or playing with kittens. Write about it here!

Energy Maps: Chakras, Meridians & More

So since we started this chapter by talking about Energy Tools and building our Symbol Library, you may be wondering — what about chakras and meridian mapping? There are many ancient systems that have been used to map out subtle energy around the human body. And it's all very helpful and accessible online. Each ancient map differs slightly, but they're all useful, depending on which one resonates most. Just as most humans have skin, bones, two arms, and legs — the same basic anatomy — we also have similar energetic anatomy, even if different countries and cultures have created different languages for referring to them.

While the various traditions may have different "maps" — that is, different ways of describing energy and the way it moves in and out and through the body — there are many similarities. I like to think that the difference has to do with cultural patterns, and the way our energy has formed as a result. When I read, I use any set of symbols that will help give me detailed information, so I use knowledge from the systems, signs, and symbols I'm familiar with — from Chinese energy meridians and natural elements to Western Astrology, Greek mythology, dream interpretation, and more! Which systems tend to speak to you or show up most in your world?

Shifting Your Reality From The Inside, Manifesting Anything

So what is one of the true gifts of having deep intuition and knowing on a daily basis? It can help us shift the circumstances of our lives. It gives us the tools to shift our external reality from the inside. Through clearing filters, we can, well, learn to see more clearly. But what happens when we're seeing clearly and we notice something we don't like? Do we have the power to change what we're sensing according to the outcome we'd prefer? Yes — we all have free will to choose and create the reality we'd like, as long as it aligns with our greater purpose. And if your filters are pretty clear, there's a very good possibility that's already happening. This is how manifestation works, in fact: "see" what sorts of energies — AKA beliefs, ideas, old stuck emotions...even a messy room — are blocking you, and then decide to clear them. Why? Remember, in order to manifest all we want, all we have to do is dissolve the blocks that have us believing that we can't. So how cool is it that you can use your tools for self-energy reading and intuition to unblock your field of vision?! It literally means you can create anything you want simply by clearing energy and then deciding to shift your intention.

As you may have noticed, there are times when your intuition leads you to the same unsavory relationship, another monotonous job, a mean boss that's just like the last mean boss...in other words, another painful lesson for clearing filters. And while it may not feel very good, I like to think there's always a reason. But consider that your intuition also leads you to a situation that builds strength, that shows you what you no longer align with, for the purpose of allowing you to choose to act differently, to create the change you'd like to see, to remove the blocks that have previously held you back?

If our beliefs shape our reality and even the intuitive clues we perceive on a daily basis, then it has to be important to challenge and change them when they no longer suit us. Which can seem impossible when we've had however many years of proof that all men act this way or all jobs are that. I know it's not always easy to believe things can be different. It's kind of like trying to make yourself believe the sun will come out this afternoon even if it's been raining every day for the last twenty years. But by noticing a spot of sun on the edge of a cloud, feeling the joy it brings, the warmth on your skin, you welcome the possibility for change. And that slowly builds up trust that change is, in fact, possible. Sort of like how we've been building our belief that we can experience energy with ease on a daily basis.

When we work with the energy of our three intuitive centers — the third eye, heart, and gut or our perception, emotion, and experience — which we've been doing this whole time, we're able to start to shift the energy or the "mindset" of each one. With that, they start to communicate with each other and they become more aligned. And again, how do you get there? Simply by using your intuition more, confirming, through experience, that it works.

How do you shift your reality? Okay, there are probably some limitations that exist, but in my experience, as long as something is totally aligned with who we are at our very core, the lessons we chose to learn in this life, anything is possible. I see it in readings all the time. The trick is to confirm this idea through experience. When you start working with energy and intuition more consciously, you'll see that you can shift your external world and its energy, by changing your internal world and its energy. At first, this takes trust in the process, some trial and error, but once you start to see results, to get the experience of it, it's incredibly empowering. And it's a little intimidating, because it means you're powerful enough to create whatever you choose, which also means being able to create any change you wish to see in the world. And that, my friends, is scary sometimes. Because it also means taking responsibility for what you see around you that you wish wasn't there. Maybe it's an unsavory office life or a person you hold accountable for everything that goes wrong. Whatever it is, the first step is to ask yourself what energy pattern you hold that may have helped create it. Sure, it's a lot easier to point outward at all the things you don't like, but it is ridiculously freeing to turn that finger around at your insides and recognize you can change anything you don't like. All through using your intuition.

Exercise: Shift Your Reality From The Inside

One evening, I was sitting in bumper-to-bumper traffic, about to teach a class, trying to think of a good example to show how shifting our energy has the power to shift our reality with the help of our intuition. I was driving a friend's car, riding the brake, when suddenly my foot slipped off it and I bumped the car in front of me. I barely noticed it, my car barely moved, but I got out anyway to make sure the couple in front of me was all right. The male driver got out of the car to assure me everything was fine. We checked the cars, we saw no damage, and he said he was okay, as was his wife. She got out of the car too, saying that she was okay, asking her husband to get back in the car and go, when she paused, looked me up and down, and said, "Actually...my neck hurts. Give me your insurance." I tried to stay calm, sensing there was something else at play. Especially since this was not the first time in my life I'd felt bullied by another woman.

I went back to my car to get the papers, holding back tears, and when I got there, my phone started playing a Bob Marley song out of nowhere: *Everything's Gonna Be Alright...No Woman, No Cry*. I burst out laughing, picked up my phone for reassurance, and just then noticed a specific sign on my phone that told me this was to do with work. That's when I remembered asking for a story to share with my class. I exhaled. Back outside, I traded numbers with the couple and wished them well. I went back home, and the next morning I did some work on my filters — the very exercise that follows. As soon as I felt my energy shift, I got a phone call. It was the woman calling to say she felt okay in the end, that she was sorry she'd been aggressive with me, and that she wished me a beautiful day.

Following is an exercise for using your intuition — your ability to look inward and read your own energy — to make profound shifts in your external reality. This is especially helpful for patterns that tend to crop up again and again, those gut-wrenching, dread-filled, oh-no-not-this-again sorts of scenarios.

To Start: Think about a situation that's nagging at you, and free-write about it on a piece of paper — all your fears, frustrations, thoughts about what's going on. Then, direct your focus inward by following the steps on the next page...

A. Keep your focus on the story you wrote about and close your eyes.

B. Touch your third eye. Notice any images, pictures, memories, beliefs, or sensations that come. Say them out loud. Keep going for 3 minutes.

C. Touch your heart. Notice any emotions, or physical sensations you feel in your body. Say them out loud. Keep going for 3 minutes.

D. Touch your belly. Keep noticing physical sensations in your body, and how they shift and move. Say them out loud. Keep going for 3 minutes.

E. Breathe, notice, speak out loud like this until you sense the energy in your body begin to feel lighter. Keep going for at least 10 minutes.

F. Note any insights that came. Then, rip up your paper and say out loud, "I am done with this story of _____ now." State out loud your insights.

…Now, ask yourself: How do you want things to go from here? Now that you've created space in your inner world, fill it up with what you want instead. Write about it here:

_____
_____
_____
_____
_____

Follow Your Feet, Follow Your Intuition

Now, since we're going to end with some of my favorite fun stories and a little bit more on energy, I'm going to wrap this chapter with one of my favorite intuitive things to do, since technically, we're talking about taking your psychic skills out into daily life, following intuition. To test it out, try following your feet. Are you ready? All you have to do is center yourself, set a timer, set an intention, then follow your feet somewhere without looking at your phone, or really paying attention to directions. I once did this in a random NYC neighborhood, asked my feet to take me to a good salad spot, and they did! It's so much fun. Now it's your turn!

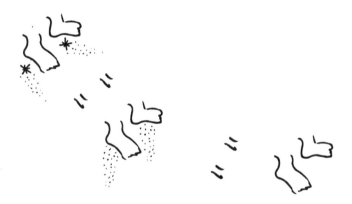

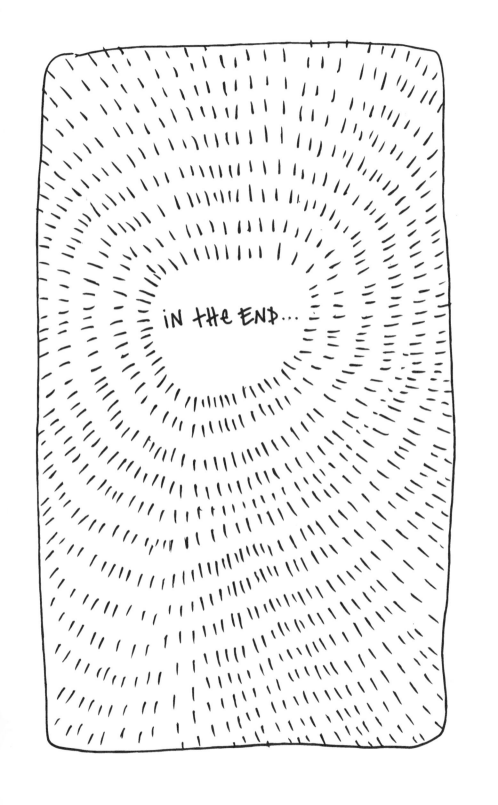

The 4,000 Page Book With All The Answers

It was Christmas-time and I was home in cold, slushy Toronto visiting family and friends. I was most of the way through the first draft of this writing when I wondered (yet again) whether to keep going. When everyone asked what I'd been up to, I'd go into a super excited rant about my book on intuition, to which I'd get deadpan stares, subject changes, and a whole bunch of, "Cool, yeah, I already know all about that." I was discouraged with the project, pretty ready to scrap it, and asked for a reason to write on.

A few days later, at lunch with my friend Tiffany and her mom, the dreaded question came up again. Now, I should mention that Tiffany is a super talented artist with a strong sense of personal direction, as is Lea, her unbelievable mom, who always knows what's going on with her kids. In other words, I was sitting with two amazingly awesome women I'd definitely think of as highly in tune with their own sense of intuition. So, thinking I had nothing new to share, I talked about the safe stuff — living, jobs, dating, friends — and left the whole book and intuition talk out of it. When I was done, Lea said, "You know, girls, sometimes I wish there was a 4,000 page book with the answers to all of life's questions." I was floored. And suddenly, I felt my charge. It was like someone had tapped me on the head and asked me to pay attention. But when I looked around, of course, no one was there. I knew this was the nudge I needed. Because if I knew I already had access to all the answers — in this case, *Should I continue this book of answers?* — why didn't they? And so I kept on, thanks to these magical angels.

The good news? This book did not turn out to be 4,000 pages, and I promise that if you practice what's in here, you will never have to lug around one that is. So what follows is a bit of encouragement for those times when you, like me, need a little tap on the head to say, "You! Yeah, you. You're doing great. Keep going!"

Little Miracles

As you may know by now, one of the best ways to come back to a place of flow is simply to remember a time when you felt it. And as you also know, my favorite way is recalling my little miracles. Someone recently asked me the craziest story of synchronicity that's happened to date. While I've seen people seem to appear out of thin air and dead rodents drop onto my doorstep after readings that had to do with uninvited pests, this one takes the cake. I still don't know what to make of it, so maybe it was for you. In that case, enjoy!

It was October 2017, and I'd stopped into a coffee shop along the Pacific Crest Trail. The first snow had fallen that morning in Lake Tahoe, and I was reminiscing about all the first snows I'd ever experienced. Having grown up in Canada, they marked a special time of year, and I was feeling pretty sentimental. I went to the local coffee shop, hoping to meet someone who was as excited about the snow as I was. And that's where I met Tyler. Originally from Florida, he'd been hiking down the American West Coast with his dad, on a road trip that started... in Canada, of course. We sat down and loved up on the snow, on Canada, chatted about our families, our sisters — his was three months pregnant, mine was having a birthday that day. I'd felt I'd met a soul brother and was grateful for the connection. We spent some time together and then went our separate ways.

Fast forward six months to Spring 2018. I happened to be on the East Coast this time, hiking along the Appalachian Trail. It was my other sister's birthday. This time I was reigning in the new growth of spring, marveling at all the sprouts with my new friend Gentry, who shared my love of the woods. She'd walked the entire Appalachian Trail and had been telling me all about it when we happened upon a beautiful couple with a baby. While we'd passed a ton of hikers and gave many of them a smile or a nod, these were the only people we'd actually talked to.

When we got back to the parking lot, there was a painted van parked right beside ours, with a license plate from Canada. "Hey," said Gentry. "I wonder if that sweet young couple was Canadian? Check out the license plate!" I would've missed it had it not been for Gentry, but the van had on it the logo of Tyler's sister's company. And I knew from Tyler that there was only one. Somehow, though none of us lived anywhere near it, I'd met Tyler's sister on the Appalachian trail. And not just on any day — on the birthday of my other sister. I texted him to share the crazy news, that I'd met his sister and family randomly in the woods that day, and that's when I realized it was on a trail with the same name as his new baby nephew. He texted back confirming that it was definitely her (I'd never met her, of course) and he told me they were en route to Canada. Which is funny because I'd met him as he was coming from there. And while there are more crazy coincidences...there are almost too many more to share, but you get it.

And I don't know what it all means right now, but, hey, mind blown all the same. And maybe that was all there was to it — just a little bit of entertainment and joyful synchronicity because I just love it so much. And since I want it all to continue, I'll say that I am open to more of it. Are you open to it too? It seems the more we all open to magic, the more it crops up everywhere and reminds us how beautiful life can be, when we allow it.

Did you just remember a fun story of a little miracle? Write it on the next page! (Not only is it a good reminder for those less-than-flowy-feeling days, but they make for really good stories at parties.)

...Write out your own little miracle here:

_____

_____

_____

_____

_____

Amplifying Energy Together

And this brings me to the topic of working energy together, or amplification. When two or more people, especially those who love and fully support each other, have the same clear focus and intention, what do you get? Energy amplified! It's why working with a loving healer can be so profound, as can the experience of going through something with a friend. It's why you may run into someone you've been thinking about again and again. Some people like to chalk it up to the Universe doing its thing, but from where I stand, I think we have more of a choice than some of us want to admit. Then again, if unconditional love is the stuff of the Universe, and it's unconditional love between humans that fuels synchronicity, I guess it's all one and the same. Maybe deep down I had really wanted to meet Tyler's nephew, and so did he (Tyler, that is — and maybe even his baby nephew) want to meet me. And so some force beyond my knowing crafted it into being.

How does this factor into developing skills for reading energy? Well, for one thing, it speaks to the power of intention, of your focus, and therefore your energy. And since the intention of this book is to develop skills for feeling into energy, since one of the most fun things about realizing your sensitive gifts is having a friend to share it with, why not double the fun, the intention, the focus, the energy, and...amplify with a friend?! If you haven't experienced it already, just wait till you see what two sensitives can create when they're working together! Because many little fishies swimming in the same direction can make such a beautiful pattern in the water.

How Do I See?

As I was sitting with my beautifully tapped-in friend, Maria, she asked me, "How do you 'see'?" She told me she sees auras around very spiritual people, especially with her eyes half open. Now, I'm a really visual person, but I don't see energy with my third eye the same as I do with my two physical ones — it's more like an overlay of something else, another reality maybe, a gentle tugging on my attention, a charge in my body that asks me to look at a character, tone, or color in another place. It doesn't happen always. But if something — maybe a guide, angel, ancestor, or even person — is present and wants to make itself known, I can feel it. All my friends feel and see the formless world differently. For instance, my friend Deidre hears things, while Sarah sees a room change color, and Marcela simply knows and speaks truth.

As I shared all this with Maria, she jumped a little, as she thought she saw a phantom puff of smoke in the corner behind me. When she told me, I laughed a little. Because this is a symbol I "see" when one of my healing guides or mentors is present during a reading. But I only ever see it with my eyes closed, and in certain situations when working with others. But here was my friend Maria seeing one of my guides in real time, with her eyes wide open! I felt so blessed. My guess is she was able to see this because she said she was curious about it, open, receptive, because we were together, fully supporting each other's experience. And it goes to show that when we're with friends who feel safe to talk about this stuff with, it opens us up to even more magic!

All of these experiences are so different for everyone. And yet I always know when I'm with a friend who's similarly sensitive because I notice that we communicate without words; when I'm with them, life just flows. And maybe that's because we let it. Because I believe the moment we decide to acknowledge the presence of the formless world of energy, to be validated in it, in all we want to experience, the magic it has to bring can make itself known.

How Do You?

It took a while to finish this book, and during that time, I saw things change dramatically. Online, everyone seemed to be talking about empaths and intuition and Reiki and subtle energy, so it became the norm. I met tons of people who were "waking up" and having enlightening experiences, frightening experiences, and experiences they just couldn't explain. One young friend I met went a whole year where she'd suddenly scream or shake involuntarily, while another had such severe pain in her bones, all she could do was sit and cry. A third friend felt she'd completely checked out, while all I heard coming out of her mouth was nothing short of the sweetest wisest tidbits of universal truth.

Yet another friend, a Stanford grad with a steady job in finance, was sitting in a board meeting when she felt herself outside of the room instead of in it. Later, traveling on a business trip, she felt herself outside again, this time on the wing of the plane. Finally, as this continued, she called in sick and took time off of work to try to "fix" whatever was wrong. And the solution came in the form of an insight that she simply hadn't been open to the full scope of her experience previously. The acceptance of this allowed her to reenter her familiar logical and structured world in a wholly new and inspiring way.

These sorts of awakenings seem to be happening more and more. And if you picked up this book because it's happening to you right now, please know that you're not alone. The opening of our perception can be sometimes blissful, sometimes painful and scary — what's happening is a shedding of what we thought we knew of the world. And when these energies are stored in the body as physical mass, as dense clumps of energy, it can feel crazy-making to move through them. And then awesome. I once passed what felt like a bowling ball of energy out my lungs during which time I could barely breathe. I was fortunate enough to be among friends who understood what was happening and took turns simply holding my body and rubbing my back. Eventually, it passed and the pain of it went away, along with the needing to know what was going on or how this fit into my "old" paradigm of beliefs about my world. After which point, more clarity came. It doesn't have to feel scary or lonely or confusing or physically difficult, but it does sometimes, and that's okay. Especially when we open our minds to all the beauty that awaits us on the other side. Which is really this side that we've been on all along. Even in all its joy and pain and polarity, this is really just the stuff of unconditional love and bliss.

This Book Was Completed Through Intuition

So just as this book was birthed through intuition, it matured in very much the same way. In writing this, I didn't always have all the answers — and I still don't — but anytime I inquired or wrote the title for a topic I felt I needed to learn, the information eventually came. It showed up via a friend, a text, the gift of a book that fell open to the page that had just the information I happened to be looking for. Other times it came through songs and unsuspecting lovely or even not-so-lovely encounters and friends. The stories played out in life, in work, in my travels, came through long and drawn out "messages" and I was sometimes randomly and blessedly invited to study with teachers who could show me the way.

I was given stories, reminded of stories, and just...so much. The more I practiced deepening my intuition, the more magical life seemed to be. As I honored my sensitivity, my natural longing to flow, life finally began to feel easy, familiar, more like it could work for me where previously it hadn't. And I was constantly reminded that I really did know just what to do, because in paying attention to all the details, I could see and therefore trust that what needed to happen already was — so long as I let it. And those snags and times I'd seemingly forgotten about the flow, about my in-tune intuition, seemed like simple reminders of how wonderful it was to be able to tap in. It's like how we can truly savor feeling happy especially after having felt sad for some time. And so, of course, I'd forget for awhile how guided I've really been, and when it came back, I'd giggle even more at the thought that I'd questioned at all. Because as it ebbed and flowed and pulled me like the tides with the moon, it truly taught me to awe and wonder at this gift that is intuition.

APPENDIX:

Plug in your energy often!

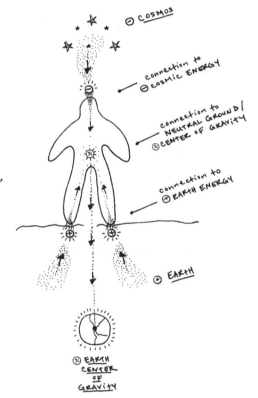

Draw energy from above, below, the energy knows where to go & harmonize it in the center, always.

...To clean, clear, release, energize, align with yourself & intuition.

Dance, Shake, Move...
clean & clear that energy!

feel feelings!

Make silly-sounding sounds!

— sss!
ch•••!
shh•••!

clean up!
(body, ♡, mind... & room!)

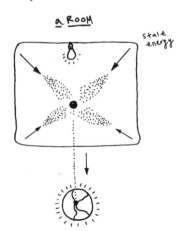

Give yourself an energy shower when needed.

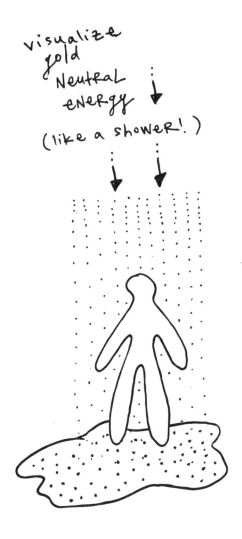

visualize gold neutral energy

(like a shower!)

Center, always center.

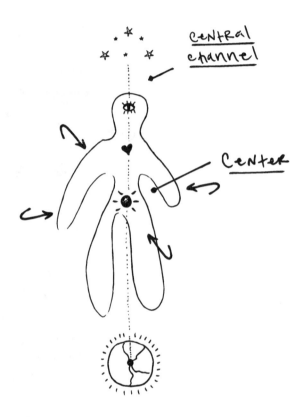

...to let your 👁
chat with ♡
chat with ☀ (gut)...

see how we are all reflections...

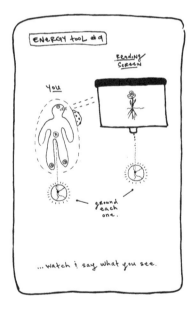

(because when we "see" others, we're really seeing ourselves.)

Amplify energy together...

— because it all starts with the thought, which ignites in our ♡ to create our physical reality. So... the more love we give it, the quicker we manifest it... together!

and last...

(but never least),

Remember

to

l♡♡♡ve

your

sensitive

soul ♡

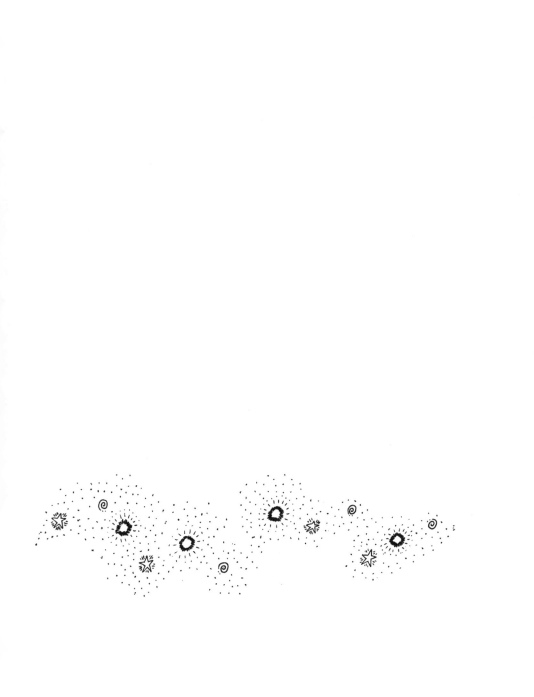

So much thanks to these angels and guides:

Mom, Dad, Jim, Allison, Dylan, Taylor, Lizzie, Veronica, Jess, Aldors, Berkovits's, and all my fam, Mamu, Evelyn, Upu George, Lea, Tiffany, Kat McCue, Marcela Urquiola, Tanya Quigley, Deidre Norman, Tasleem Visram, Jen Law, Eryn Treanor, Kelly Spence, Maria Leiber, Cristalle, Sarah, Joe Albert, Anna Joseph, Ethan Corfield, Amy Needles, Britta Hanson, Pat Davis, Trent Mayer, Chandika Devi, Angelica Radicinski, Petros, Alessandra Gallo, Cecille Wong, Marisa Hahn, Aeja Goldsmith, Debra Lynne Katz, Uma Dinsmore-Tulli, Minke De Vos, Ford Peck, Eli Cohen, Michael Winn, Dr Ng, Lee Holden, deAnna Batdorff, Sarafina Fornara, Garrett Brill, Audrey Brown, Nathalie Arbel, Ben, Devaya, Oded, M Reid, many bathtubs around the world, all the people who dare to be themselves, and every Phoenix I've met on this wild journey.

Courtney Alex Aldor is an intuitive channel, writer, artist, and all-out Qigong nerd. When she's not dancing her way around the globe, you can find her sitting under a tree near her home in beautiful Marin County, California.

For more info: **www.CourtneyAlex.com**
Or follow her on IG: **@tiny_psychic**

Made in United States
Troutdale, OR
01/23/2024

16995572R10186